SELF-TALK

The exploration of self-talk brings us to the core of child-rearing and teaching children. The approaches traditionally used have emphasized external control, external rewards—techniques that are used *on* children rather than techniques the children can use themselves. Teaching children to talk to themselves in vital and helpful ways will be a central force for allowing them to grow up with a sense of inner inspiration, self-control, and internal standards.

Much of the negative self-talk children learn is assimilated from adults: "I can't take this"; "You'll pay for that"; "You're lazy." The remark doesn't have to be about the child in order for it to become a part of his or her self-talk repertoire; but if the observations, whatever they're about, are negative, children will often begin to tell themselves the same things.

Learning to use self-talk in a *positive* way takes work, but it is an exciting and rewarding process, and the results are worth the effort. In fact, teaching a child to use positive self-talk is an investment not only in his or her development, but also in the ways you will relate to each other in the future.

St. Martin's Paperbacks titles are available at quantity discounts for sales promotions, premiums or fund raising. Special books or book excerpts can also be created to fit specific needs.

For information write to special sales manager, St. Martin's Press, 175 Fifth Avenue, New York, N.Y. 10010.

"I THINK I CAN, I KNOW I CAN!"

USING SELF-TALK TO HELP RAISE CONFIDENT, SECURE KIDS

Susan Isaacs and Wendy Ritchey, Ph.D.

ST. MARTIN'S PAPERBACKS

NOTE: If you purchased this book without a cover you should be aware that this book is stolen property. It was reported as 'unsold and destroyed' to the publisher, and neither the author nor the publisher has received any payment for this 'stripped book'.

"I THINK I CAN, I *KNOW* I CAN!"

Copyright © 1989 by Susan Isaacs and Wendy Ritchey.

Cover photograph courtesy of Superstock, Inc.

All rights reserved. No part of this book may be used or reproduced in any manner whatsoever without written permission except in the case of brief quotations embodied in critical articles or reviews. For information address St. Martin's Press, 175 Fifth Avenue, New York, N.Y. 10010.

Library of Congress Catalog Card Number: 89-32766

ISBN: 0-312-92678-2

Printed in the United States of America

St. Martin's Press hardcover edition published 1989
St. Martin's Paperbacks edition/December 1991

10 9 8 7 6 5 4 3 2 1

To Jim,
our guide and
inspiration

Contents

	Acknowledgments	ix
1	Teaching Kids Positive Self-Talk	1
2	Five Steps for Helping a Child Learn Positive Self-Talk	12
3	Advanced Techniques for Changing Self-Talk	38
4	Keeping Anger Under Control	56
5	Overcoming Fears	75
6	Supercharging Learning	94
7	Self-Talk and Sports and Games	114
8	Making Friends	127
9	Friendships in Late Childhood and Adolescence	153
10	Self-Talk and Health	173
	Conclusion	191
	Bibliography	193
	Index	195

Acknowledgments

We want to give heartfelt thanks to all those who helped make this book possible: Wendy's husband, Scott Wallace, for contributing everything from editing to childcare; Dr. Carol Weyland, for consultation and inspiration; Alice Cutteridge, Matt Isaacs, and the Italias for aiding so substantially in our research; Bob Royeton, Mimi Drake, and Adelle De Persia for reading and commenting on portions of the manuscript; Collins Flannery for skillful editing; Jeff Kohl, for technical advice; and Susan's daughters, Gabrielle and Mari, for supporting our efforts in so many creative ways.

We want to give special appreciation to our agent, Ruth Cohen, for believing in the book and for working so hard with such high professional standards on its behalf, and to our editor, Barbara Anderson, for her patience and perceptive editing.

·1·
TEACHING KIDS POSITIVE SELF-TALK

• • •

A year after she had adjusted happily to preschool, four-year-old Dana went through a change. She suddenly started clinging to her mother when they got to school and protesting that she didn't want her to go. After discussing the problem at length with Dana and among themselves, Dana's teachers and parents could find no reason for her behavior. Nor could they do anything about it. In spite of all reassurances, Dana's irrational crying continued. After weeks of having to peel off Dana at the classroom door, Dana's mother consulted a child psychologist. He concluded that some incident must have set off Dana's fears, but now they seemed to have a life of their own. He said she would outgrow them. But Dana's mother didn't know if she wanted to wait that long. Her own sanity seemed at risk when she thought of weeks or months of dealing with Dana's clingy behavior. She felt there must be a practical way to help Dana to help herself. And then she stumbled across it.

• • • 2 • • •

She read an article on positive self-talk and its potential for helping adults and children with all kinds of difficult problems.

WHAT IS SELF-TALK?

Self-talk is the phrase psychologists have coined for the ways we direct ourselves to relate to the world. Although we may not be aware of it, we all talk to ourselves—sometimes out loud and sometimes internally—and many of our feelings and attitudes toward life are conditioned by the things we say.

Self-talk varies from casual remarks like "I don't have to take that" to full-scale dialogues in which we debate whether to get married or take a new job. Our self-talk is so automatic and ingrained that we don't even notice it. That's why few of us are aware of the power that it exercises over our lives.

However, the study of self-talk has permeated such fields as psychology, neuropsychology, education, and sports psychology. In a recent study by Dr. Paul Horton, a psychoanalyst who is an expert in the area of solace, self-talk was identified as one of the crucial remedies people use in times of turmoil and grief.

Psychologist Dr. Shad Helmstetter refers to *positive* self-talk as the most powerful force humans have for self-transformation. In an exhaustive analysis of self-help literature, Helmstetter identified three basic weaknesses in these books and the techniques they describe: (1) the solutions presented lack permanance; (2) the authors apparently lack an understanding of the physiological processes of the human brain based on what we know about mind/brain functions; and (3) the recommended methods do not teach the ability to program the subconscious-mind, the control center of the brain. Helmstetter states that the only tool that includes all three of these attributes is self-talk.

Scientists believe that self-talk provides a kind of program that our subconscious minds respond to. Our minds work something like computers: Our brains are the hardware, and what we say to ourselves is the software. Although we are seldom aware of it, even the most casual admonitions we make to ourselves can make a strong impression on our minds, depending on the emotional power they hold for us.

Some of the power of these impressions is explained by new findings in brain research. Scientists have found that the brain cannot distinguish between a real experience and an imaginary one. In other words, when we picture ourselves sucking a lemon, we automatically salivate to neutralize imaginary acid in our mouths. When we talk to ourselves, we produce signals in our brains (especially if that talking is accompanied by visual images) and our bodies respond by producing chemicals that affect our feelings and behavior.

This process has been widely documented in the areas of health and stress. When people tell themselves that an event is threatening or beyond their control, or that they are unable to cope with it, the body responds as if it is under attack. Another person may tell himself something positive about the same event ("I'm not going to let this bother me") and experience a neutral or positive reaction. Studies also show that when people tell themselves that they are going to get sick, or when they consider themselves types who get sick easily, they are more likely to develop illnesses.

••• 4 •••

CHANGING NEGATIVE SELF-TALK
INTO POSITIVE SELF-TALK

The most exciting findings, however, are that self-talk can be transformed in both adults and children to enhance their lives and help them solve troublesome problems. Dana's case is a good example. Her mother wasn't able to discover what had caused Dana's sudden anxiety about school, but she did notice that the things Dana said seemed to perpetuate and escalate that fear: "I know you'll never come back"; "I'll be left all alone."

The article Dana's mother read suggested that by altering someone's self-talk, you could help them to change their feelings and behavior. Since Dana's mother was becoming desperate, she gave it a try. She began to teach Dana to make reassuring statements to herself—"Someone will always be there to pick me up"; "I will be happy at school while mother is gone." Practicing these statements was presented as a game to Dana, and she was an eager player. In only a few weeks' time, her behavior was noticeably improved.

Separation anxiety is only one issue that can be dramatically affected by constructive self-talk. Psychologists have shown that teaching children this positive approach can turn even the toughest problems around in record time, problems that would previously have taken months or years of therapy if they ever were resolved at all. A growing body of evidence suggests that changing a child's self-talk is often the treatment of choice. More important, that treatment can be taught by parents, teachers, and other concerned adults. It is simple and often brings dramatic results.

For example, positive self-talk has sometimes proved as effective as medication in treating hyperactivity in children. It has also proved especially useful in helping children who have problems with self-control, aggressiveness, fears, and phobias.

And self-talk can be powerful in other ways. It has assisted children in school settings to learn successfully and to make friends more easily. Through positive self-talk children are being taught to expand their capacities to learn, to improve their social attitudes and behavior, to enhance their athletic abilities, to relax, and to program themselves for good health. Some schools have introduced new curricula that include the use of positive self-talk for students of all ages, from preschool to high school.

THE BENEFITS OF STARTING EARLY

Such efforts reflect a growing belief that starting the use of positive self-talk early can make a pivotal difference in the lives of young children. Dr. Shad Helmstetter, who is in the process of setting up self-talk centers all over the country, estimates that 75 percent of adult self-talk is negative, holding people back from accomplishing what they want in life. If children can learn to use positive self-talk early, their potential for growth in every area of life might be expanded in ways we can't even imagine. If they learn to motivate themselves to achieve through positive self-talk, they have one of the most powerful tools available for self-actualization.

Scientists have discovered that the brain's right and left hemispheres have distinct functions. The left hemisphere, which is responsible for logical, rational, and linear thought, becomes dominant by the time we reach adulthood. In early childhood, however, the right hemisphere, from which creativity, intuition, humor, and imagination spring, is used equally with the left brain. Self-talk, a left-brain function, is enhanced by coupling it with visualization. Childhood is an ideal time to teach these techniques, since the right-brain skill of visualization is more active during this stage of development.

THE ROOTS OF SELF-TALK

The development of self-talk is a natural process that should aid development rather than detract from it. Scientists have found that inner speech begins in early childhood, when a baby learns to talk by imitating the sounds around him. That early "talk" is self-stimulating. The baby listens to himself as well as others. When he makes sounds, he stimulates himself to talk more. We usually think of talking as being related to communication, but language specialists have documented the existence of a whole separate track of language called egocentric speech. Egocentric speech refers to the language the child uses to talk to himself, at first out loud and later internally. This self-talk helps to determine the child's reactions and feelings and is pivotal in the formation of self-control, learning, problem solving, and moral development. In fact, when there are problems in these areas, they often relate to a deficit in the development of self-talk that needs to be corrected.

The exploration of self-talk brings us to the core of child-rearing and teaching children. The approaches we have traditionally used emphasize external control, external rewards—techniques that are used *on* the child rather than techniques he can use himself. Teaching children to talk to themselves in vital and helpful ways will be a central force for allowing them to grow up with a sense of inner inspiration, self-control, and internal standards.

By tuning in to children's self-talk we will also become more sensitive about our interactions and how we can best support children's growth. Much of the negative self-talk children learn is assimilated from adults: "I can't take this"; "You'll pay for that"; "You're lazy." The remark doesn't have to be about the child in order for it to become a part of his self-talk repertoire; most of us comment on the events of life or predict how things will turn out. If these observations are negative, children will often begin to tell themselves the same things.

When we start paying attention to a child's self-talk, we can't help but listen to our own, hearing the ways we determine our own attitudes and reactions by instructing ourselves or debating with ourselves either internally or out loud.

Learning to use self-talk positively takes some work, but it is an exciting and rewarding process at any age. The steps and techniques we outline here will help you to relate better to the children you know. You will inevitably become a more supportive parent, teacher, grandparent, or friend. But these techniques will affect your life, too. You can't learn about self-talk without its affecting your sense of self and the way you approach life.

In the next chapter we will outline five simple steps for exploring the use of positive self-talk with children. We suggest that you read those steps once over lightly and experiment a little. The following chapter introduces you to more involved techniques that have proved effective for changing everything from a child's self-image to his athletic prowess. Then go on and read the next chapters on applying self-talk to challenging areas of life. Getting into the nitty-gritty of using it in everyday situations will make things more concrete. Then you can go back to those five basic steps and try to apply them to real-life situations more effectively.

THE FIVE MOST-ASKED QUESTIONS ABOUT SELF-TALK

You probably have some questions at this point. Here are some of the most common questions people ask us about these issues.

1. At what age can you try to work with a child's self-talk? It seems like an approach that might work only with older children.

Positive self-talk isn't just for older children, but we have to play different roles with children at different stages. When children are very young, before the age of about four, our awareness of the techniques should help us to program positive voices in children. As you go through the book you will see constant references to the ways that we can support positive self-talk through our own modeling.

When a child reaches the age of three or four, you can also begin to introduce the idea of self-talk and how it can help or hinder the ways one feels. But these ideas must be kept very simple. At this stage, children are just learning to identify and have words for feelings. You might explain that saying certain things to himself can make a child feel scared, angry, sad, or happy. You can give examples of things children say, and their effects. When a child is feeling scared or unhappy, you can suggest that he say specific phrases designed to reassure himself. Children can start saying affirmations to themselves at bedtime (more on this in the next chapter.) They can also begin to use self-talk as a crucial mechanism for self-control. But they aren't yet capable of carrying out on their own any of the more sophisticated techniques that you will find outlined in the next chapters.

In elementary school, children can really learn to use self-talk effectively. They have greater ability to concentrate and experiment. However, the important thing to keep in mind with elementary-school children and adolescents is that they have to be receptive and motivated to try out these experiments. They can't be pressured or forced to do so. When you change self-talk you are really changing your process of thought and your abilities to use your mind effectively, and the motivation and commitment to do that has to come from within. Once children see the ways self-talk can help give them greater "mind power," they are eager to try new possibilities.

2. Isn't using self-talk complicated?

Negative voices might suggest that trying to change self-talk is a big deal, but it really isn't. Those voices defend against change. Learning to talk positively to oneself isn't an instant solution to every problem. And it does take time, especially if it has been preceded by years of self-defeating self-talk. That's why working with children can be so gratifying. There is less to "undo." The research evidence seems to show that the possibilities are endless. In the following chapter, you will explore ways to tune in to self-talk and help children use it to their advantage.

3. How do I know using positive self-talk will work? Isn't it just another self-help technique like the countless others on psychology and parenting I hear about?

You don't know that it will work, and there are no guarantees. But usually people have a feeling about its power even if they haven't thought much about it. When they start to read about it the whole process makes sense on an intuitive level. The difference between working with self-talk and many other available programs for personal change is that the techniques introduced here have been proved effective by psychological researchers and clinicians over years of study. In fact, working with self-talk is seen as one of the quickest and most effective remedies for many pressing problems.

4. What if a child doesn't want to talk about what he says to himself? What if he thinks the whole idea is stupid or not worth his while?

If children don't want to talk about self-talk, don't push them. Knowing how inner speech works will be a valuable resource for you as a person and as a parent or teacher (or whatever your role might be with children.) Concentrate on developing your own positive self-talk and watch the effects. Share that process with those around you, including children. If you don't pressure them to participate in this process, they will gradually open up to the ideas on some level, even if they never show it. On the other hand, if you present some of the experiments outlined here as games, most children will be eager to try them. Just be careful to praise them for their efforts and encourage them to continue the "games" because any kind of change takes work.

5. Is self-talk just a "Band-Aid" approach? What if a child has deeper problems and really needs professional help? Could I actually harm a child through trying these techniques?

11

Self-talk isn't intended to be a substitute for counseling. Positive self-talk can help anyone, but it shouldn't be viewed as a panacea for any problem, no matter how severe. Children sometimes need specialists to help them work through particular problems. A child with learning difficulties may need a specialist to design a program for her, but your use of positive self-talk can augment those efforts, especially if you share it with a specialist. A child or adolescent with problems that interfere with his normal functioning socially, emotionally, academically, or physically should be seen by a child therapist who can determine his needs. Self-talk can enhance the efforts of the therapist, but it is best to consult with him to make sure you are working in harmony with his goals.

Helping patients think and feel more positively about themselves is almost always one of the goals of psychotherapy, but there are numerous "paths"—or theories and approaches—toward reaching that goal. Working directly to change what a patient says to himself is an accepted and increasingly common approach in child and adult psychotherapy; but it is not the only approach. Even if your youngster is in therapy with someone who does not use these methods, he might benefit from being exposed to them as long as he is not pressured to change his self-talk or made to feel bad about himself.

·2·
FIVE STEPS FOR HELPING A CHILD LEARN POSITIVE SELF-TALK

• • •

Like anything else, learning the techniques for using positive self-talk takes work. But the results are worth the effort. In fact, teaching a child to use self-talk is an investment not only in his development, but also in the ways you will relate to each other in the future. Putting effort into these steps will make a positive change in your perspective.

STEP 1: LOOK AT YOUR OWN SELF-TALK

Most people don't realize how often their reactions are immediately affected by their self-talk. An understanding of this can even explain apparent differences between people. For example, thirty-two-year-old Annie, a mother of two, is always nervous. Any little event in life seems to set her worrying. She consistently says things like, "What if this happens?" "How am I going to cope?" "With my luck, it will turn out terrible."

On the other hand, twenty-eight-year-old Joyce, a mother of three, is pretty relaxed and matter-of-fact about life. She tends to use humor to cope with crises and seldom seems thrown by what comes up.

Is there a basic difference in these women's temperaments? Perhaps. But every day Annie has a challenge to deal with that Joyce does not. Her inner voices continually tell her that things will turn out disastrously and that she won't be able to cope. Annie's family and friends always try to support and reassure her. But their voices aren't so persuasive or powerful as her own inner voices. That's because those negative voices developed when Annie was so young that she hardly knows they exist. Most of us grow up with some negative voices that we are scarcely aware of. The sad thing for Annie is that she never developed positive voices strong enough to overbalance the other ones.

Joyce's self-talk is not free of negative inner voices, but as a child she was supported in developing positive ones. In Joyce's inner dialogues those positive voices tend to dominate, giving her an entirely different road map for life. They are encouraging: They tell her to relax, assure her that everything will turn out fine, remind her that she can handle anything that comes along. People see Joyce's relaxed manner and enjoy being around her. If they thought about it they might assume that Joyce's life is pretty much stress-free.

But that's not true. In fact, the stressors in Joyce's life might be assessed as greater than those in Annie's. However, her inner voices program her to react in different ways.

You may not have tuned in to the fact that you have many different interior voices. In *The Inner Enemy* Dr. George Bach explains:

> Most people are aware that they are always thinking on some level, even if they can't always pin down their thoughts or make sense of what's going through their heads. What they don't realize is that there is not just one person—a monolithic me—talking in there. But many *me*s. They fail to see the obvious: that the self that says you look wonderful in that green dress can't be the same self that says in the next breath that no one will be interested in talking to you at the party. Or that the supportive voice that congratulates you on making that difficult phone call can't be the same voice that neglects to tell you (as it usually does) to watch out for that low shelf when you stand up from the phone. Or that the inner voice telling you that it's time to have a baby is not the same one that says, "But then I'll never write that master's thesis."

When we start to listen to our self-talk, we can begin to hear the dialogues that go on within ourselves—dialogues that determine our reactions and attitudes and shape many of our decisions. This tuning in to inner voices can actually give us a much more vivid and accurate picture of our inner lives than can thinking in terms of a self or pondering what we are really like.

You can begin to get to know some of those voices by paying attention to what you say internally in a variety of situations. Try listening to your internal speech when you do the following:

- make a mistake,
- try on new clothes,
- wonder if you should bring up a conflicting situation to someone,
- are about to take a risk,
- get your feelings hurt,
- feel angry and wonder what to do,
- are anticipating the outcome of something,
- are wondering whether to go on diet,
- are trying to decide whether to buy something,
- are trying to learn something new.

We can make self-talk more audible by paying attention to our dialogues in these situations. But tuning in to self-talk is a little like trying to work a shortwave radio. We are more apt to get results if we tune in when there is some action—something for us to hear. Some situations generate more self-talk than do others. They are usually situations that involve duality—when we have conflicting desires or views, when we feel insecure but want to do something about it, when we feel angry but don't know how to express it, when we are trying to make a hard decision.

Our inner voices become more audible and distinguishable in those situations. If we put some effort into listening to our "selves," those voices start to take on a character of their own.

Do you have an encourager? a complainer? a doomsayer? an inflamer?

Different voices tend to predominate in different people. Annie's worrier and doomsayer have an upper hand in her internal dialogues, while in Joyce's inner speech her reassurer and encourager tend to keep her relaxed and on top of things. The voices that tend to dominate Annie's thinking hold her back in life. They keep her from growing and becoming the kind of person she has the potential to be. Everyone has to have negative voices, and when, like Annie, you aren't aware of their destructive power, you are at their mercy.

Becoming aware of those voices and the actual words you use in inner dialogue can release potential for change. It can also help you to understand others and support their abilities to change. As you begin to notice the voices in the people around you—children and adults—you will hear encouraging, self-enhancing, reassuring voices and self-limiting, discouraging, and even destructive ones. The first step with yourself and with others is just to observe. Inner voices are tricky. You have to be patient in order to identify them. It is not possible even to begin to get to know them unless you are willing just to listen without judging, jumping to conclusions, or trying to make a change. Speaking of listening leads us to our next step.

STEP 2: OBSERVE THE CHILD'S SELF-TALK

Now that you've had some experience, you're ready to tune in to the child's self-talk. Since you don't have the benefit of being inside the child's head, you have to make some educated guesses. Listening carefully to what he says to himself aloud and what he says to others about his experiences, as well as watching what he *does* in various situations, will provide useful cues to what kinds of things he's saying internally.

At this point, try to resist the temptation to change what he says to himself. Just listen, watch, and begin to form some hypotheses about what may be going on inside his head.

••• 17 •••

LISTEN TO HIS SELF-SPEECH

Our usual way of listening to language is as a form of communication between people. But all language isn't aimed at communicating. As previously mentioned, a form of speech develops during the preschool years that is composed of talk for talk's sake. It is called egocentric speech because children essentially talk to themselves. A child playing with blocks or in a sandbox often talks to herself as if she is oblivious to those around her.

At about the age of seven, much of this speech is internalized, but it doesn't go away. What was formerly said out loud now goes on inside the child's head. But older children still talk to themselves out loud at times, and the habit continues into adulthood.

You can probably get in touch with your own tendency to talk out loud to yourself if you think of the following situations:

- walking around your house looking for something you've lost,
- realizing that you aren't doing a recipe right and going back over it again,
- making a mistake on a report that you're writing,
- trying to figure out an error in your checkbook,
- getting lost while driving and trying to trace your route,
- being interrupted in the middle of a task and trying to reorient yourself to continue.

Listen to what the child is saying out loud to himself about his reactions to situations and the people around him, to the tasks before him, and to his feelings (anger, fear, frustration, elation). Don't be dismayed by the number of negative or discouraging statements you may hear. Everyone makes negative statements and it is nothing to become alarmed about. Since we don't usually acknowledge the power of such statements, they don't usually capture our attention. But don't try to correct the child or show your reactions to what he is saying. The idea is to become aware of the typical voices a child uses and the phrases that tend to be repeated by those voices in particular situations.

Jot down what you hear. Be especially alert to red flags that suggest negative, self-limiting messages and note when they tend to occur. For instance, "I *can't* do it," "He *should* give it to me," "It's not *fair*," or "I *have* to" can be indicators that a child is feeling helpless, or compelled to act in certain ways. All children say things like this sometimes. But repeated red-flag statements indicate that certain ways of reacting have become a pattern.

Other phrases suggest the child is overgeneralizing or filtering so that he sees only part of the true picture. Doing this makes things seem absolute and worse than they really are. Reality is actually distorted when one say things like, "*No one* wants to play with me"; "I know it's going to turn out *terrible*"; "If that happens, I won't be able to *stand* it"; "It *always* ends up awful."

You might also listen for labels the child uses for other people and herself. These labels create not only attitudes but also behavior. They distort the way children see others or themselves. If you hear phrases like "I'm so *stupid*," "He's a *dork*," "She's *mean*," "He's *unfair*," you know the child is programming herself for failure and disappointment.

Of course, you also want to be alerted to the child's use of positive, empowering words. Note when the child uses phrases like "I bet I *can* do it," "I want to *decide*," "It's my *choice*," and the effects these seem to have on her.

As you listen to the concrete words a child uses, you may get a picture of some inner voices. Do you hear an encourager that helps a child when he is down? Is there a discourager that jumps in whenever the going gets rough and tells him a task isn't worth doing or that he isn't up to doing it? Does the child you're observing have an inflamer that tends to make her more and more angry in situations? Or a doomsayer who convinces her that things will turn out badly and makes her worry? Those voices emerge in the things a child says to himself in various situations.

LISTEN TO WHAT HE SAYS TO OTHERS

Listen carefully to what he says to others for cues about what he's saying to himself. Listen for the same red flags you may have heard in his self-speech (words like *have to*, *can't*, *unfair*, *terrible*, *never*, and *always*) as well as the same empowering words (*can*, *try*, *want to*, *choose to*). Jot down what he says without his being aware of it; you don't want to make him self-conscious.

What you hear the child say to herself out loud or to others may not sound especially negative, but remember that what we hear a child say is just the tip of the iceberg. Self-talk tends to be much more repetitious than external talk. For example, when you are anxious you might say, "What if this happens? I couldn't stand it." If you say it aloud, you usually get feedback. Someone might say, "Oh, don't worry, everything will turn out all right" and that response makes it seem inappropriate to keep repeating the litany. But that feedback loop doesn't operate with internal speech. Anxious people will probably continue to say to themselves "What if this happens?" over and over, since there is no internal feedback to check them. That unchecked repetition then becomes a trigger for increasing feelings of anxiety, or anger, or whatever they may be feeling.

WATCH WHAT THE CHILD DOES

In order to get a clearer idea of the effects of your child's self-talk, jot down not only what he does, but also the effects of what he says. For example, "Gives up on math assignment as soon as he starts saying that his homework is boring or it's not fair that he has so much," or "Perks up when he says, 'I bet I can do it' and keeps trying."

It is necessary to observe a child and some of the ways her self-talk affects her before you can begin to think about making changes. At first this may be difficult. You may want to jump in and point out all the negative effects she is having on herself. But this will only make her resist your suggestions and put up a wall that will reinforce negative habits.

STEP 3: INTRODUCE THE CONCEPT OF SELF-TALK

Once you've examined your own self-talk and have begun to observe your child, the next step is to introduce the idea of self-talk to your children, and engage them in thinking about it.

When you do so, keep it simple. A most effective way to

introduce the idea is to share your explorations into your own self-talk and what you have discovered about its effects on you.

To a child who has been frightened you might say, "You know, when I was a child I used to tell myself scary things when I was lying in bed at night. I would say, 'What if a monster comes out of the closet?' or 'I bet that's someone tapping on my window.' We all talk to ourselves inside. Sometimes we say things that make us feel happy and safe and other times we get ourselves more scared by the things we say. Do you ever say things to yourself that make you worried or afraid?"

To a child who is upset about a friend you might say, "When I was a child and something happened with my best friend, sometimes I would go home and tell myself she was mean, and she didn't like me anymore, and she was unfair. Those things would make me madder and madder at my friend when what I really wanted to do was to make up. There's nothing wrong with being mad but sometimes we don't want to stay mad and the things we say to ourselves keep us feeling that way. Sometimes we calm ourselves down by talking but other times we can get ourselves madder and madder. Do you ever say things to yourself that make you angrier and angrier at someone?"

You can also use examples from your current self-talk to introduce the subject. To a child who is procrastinating about doing a homework assignment you might say, "You know, sometimes when I don't want to do something I keep telling myself about all the other things I want to be doing. I say, 'It's not fair that I can't be watching TV like everybody else.' Or I tell myself how hard doing it will be, and it makes it harder for me to get started. Do you ever talk to yourself ahead of time about how hard something is going to be?"

In addition to the examples from your own life, you can also draw on your observations of your children as an introduction to self-talk.

You might say, "You know, I noticed how you sometimes say, 'I bet I can do it' right before you're going to try something new like swinging from a rope or doing an acrobatic trick. That's the way athletes talk to themselves before they do something hard. We all talk to ourselves inside; telling ourselves we can do something actually makes us better able to do it."

Although the idea of having different voices in our heads would be confusing to young children, the idea can be helpful to older children and adolescents. You might say, "I know when I'm about to do something new, I often hear this little voice inside me that says, 'You'll never be able to do it. Why even try?' so I get discouraged before I even start. We have different voices inside of us that tell us things at different times. Do you ever have a voice that holds you back from doing something exciting and hard?"

When an adolescent is having a social problem, instead of telling him what to do, you could use the idea of self-talk to help him gain a new understanding.

You might say, "I know how you're feeling. It's hard to go up to someone you don't know and ask them out. I know when I'm going to try to introduce myself to someone new I talk to myself about it first. I might tell myself that I think they are probably feeling kind of alone, too, and they'd probably like to talk to someone. I persuade myself that I can make them feel good by going up and introducing myself. When I tell myself that, I feel so much more confident. I wondered if you ever try talking to yourself when you're feeling nervous with someone."

Adolescents can understand some of the complexities of self-talk and may enjoy reading about its potential for changing their lives. You might recommend a book to them such as *What to Say When You Talk to Your Self* by Dr. Shad Helmstetter. This is a delightful, easy-to-understand book that can help an adolescent tune into himself. It can also provide the basis for conversation between the two of you.

STEP 4: MODEL POSITIVE SELF-TALK

Much of the self-talk a child engages in will be based on the actual words he has heard adults say. Phrases that parents or teachers use without thinking, like, "You're lazy," or "How could you do such a thing?" or "You're going to get it for that" get programmed into a child's inner voices and tend to play again and again.

As you become aware of self-talk, one of the most exciting things you can do is to help program children's interior voices to be positive, encouraging, nurturing, and realistic. You can program children to learn better, relax more, and control their negative impulses, as well as to feel better about themselves, through consciously modeling what self-talk can be.

You can begin to do this by noticing what you say out loud in specific situations. There are four types of situations that are particularly potent in the formation of a child's self-talk:

1. teaching talk: situations that involve talking to a child or demonstrating how something is done;
2. controlling talk: situations that involve controlling your own impulses (anger, for example) in front of a child or attempting to control or discipline him;

3. coping and nurturing talk: situations that involve coping with stress or nurturing yourself or others;
4. future talk: situations that involve focusing on the outcome of events in the future.

Teaching talk

Whenever you show a child how to do something or help him solve a problem, you develop and reinforce the voice of his "instructor." That voice is crucial for leading him through learning tasks on his own. When Ronnie was teaching her son James to bake a cake, she talked about each step she used: separating egg yolks from whites, creaming shortening, sifting flour, and blending all the other ingredients. When nine-year-old James tried to bake a cake himself, he repeated those steps out loud so that he could do it just the way his mother had.

The better you are at patiently breaking tasks into small steps, and encouraging a child to try without fear of mistakes, the better he will be able to teach himself (see Chapter 6, on learning).

Controlling talk

Type One:

"How could you do such a thing?"
"You're going to get it."

Type Two:

"If you make fun of other people, they won't want to play with you."
"If you play with your food, you'll have to leave the table."

Research shows that the two approaches to discipline in the examples above affect children in very different ways. The first type of talk controls through force and tends to develop angry voices in children. Rather than making children compliant, it may develop the voice of the bully or inflamer.

The child who is warned, "I'm going to punish you for that" learns to say the same thing to himself about others, and these provocative words are likely to incite him to aggression. When nine-year-old John is confronted by someone on the playground, his inner voices repeat things he has heard that trigger his rage: "You're just trying to get to me," or "I'll show you." While most of his classmates have learned to mediate situations by saying things internally like, "I know if I fight I'll just get in trouble myself," John actually feels helpless regarding controlling his impulses.

The second type of self-talk models internal control through reasoning, empathizing, and foreseeing the consequences. When children have the benefit of these models, they can gradually develop true self-control. They don't need to be controlled because they can control themselves. If you can consciously try to discipline children in ways that help them reason and predict the consequences of their actions, you will program them for developing the voices of a reasoner and internal mediator.

The talk that adults model when they themselves experience a conflict is also important.

Ten-year-old Adam's father is a contractor. Adam often went to construction sites with him to watch new projects. Although Adam never saw his dad actually hit one of the workers, he often heard him threaten to do so. Adam's father had two conflicting voices in his own internal talk, an inflamer that made him react with a short fuse and a reasoner that kept his temper in check. But since Adam's dad wasn't aware of the model he was providing, he would tend to blow off steam by talking about his angry feelings. Adam never heard the voice of the reasoner that helped his father to calm down and empathize with others. If his father had been conscious of modeling effective self-talk, he could have helped his son to develop his own self-control more effectively.

Adam needed help to be able to control his temper and the school recommended counseling. Fortunately, Adam's therapist was schooled in self-talk and was able to model the voice of the reasoner for Adam. She showed him how she would talk to herself in order to stop, think, plan, and act to control her temper. Adam learned to use those same steps to talk himself through controlling his temper.

Coping and nurturing talk

"Don't worry, I can handle it."
"I'm not going to worry about it, I can only do my best."
"I've been working hard and I'm going to take a break."
"I can't take much more."
"This is going to be a terrible day."
"I need a drink, I can't take much more."

These statements illustrate various ways in which adults respond to stress and program children to do the same. When adults make statements that demonstrate their belief that they can cope, children learn to develop the voices of the reassurer and coper. When you talk out loud about taking care of your needs and not pushing yourself too far, you help children to develop inner voices that can nurture them when you're not around. A child who learns to make nurturing statements to himself is more apt to know when he needs to slow down, eat, rest, and relax.

Conversely, chronic health problems are associated with an inability to nurture oneself. If a child assimilates the voice of the slave driver from the adults around him, he is apt to admonish himself to go faster, and ignore his bodily signals. Since research is showing that many of our epidemic health problems actually begin with childhood responses to stress, the development of these inner voices seems crucial.

In order to discern the way different perspectives affect your bodily state, try making the following statements out loud and chronicling your responses.

"I feel completely relaxed."
"My whole body is at peace."
"I'm going to take care of myself today."
"I'm going to eat a wonderful meal."

"I'm really upset."
"My whole body feels anxious and tense."
"I'm going to run myself ragged."
"I'm going to eat as fast as I can."

Thinking about the model you provide in managing tension is the first step in being able to help the children around you to handle the stresses in their lives. During difficult times it's often hard to monitor our reactions, let alone what we say. But if you start to think of the importance of what you say as well as its effect on you and those around you, you can begin to change your own reaction to adversity. This process can transform your ability to cope. It is important to remember that it is not the event itself that provides the stress but your reaction to it.

Future talk

Adults are often unaware of the predictions they make about how life will unfold in the future:

"It's going to be a disaster."
"I'll never get that raise."
"Things are bound to get better."
"I'm sure everything will be fine."

Adults frequently make predictions about children, too:

"You'll never win if you don't practice."
"You're going to make a mess of it."
"No one will want to play with you if you act like that."

In making predictions, one influences one's approach to situations and one's confidence to deal with them. Adults are usually unaware that the predictions they make develop voices in the children around them. The doomsayer chronically predicts catastrophe. The inspirer infuses enthusiasm and foretells positive outcomes. Positive attitudes that cynics call "Pollyannaish" actually produce the voice of the inspirer and build its strength.

It wasn't until her fifteen-year-old daughter came home in tears that Erin realized the way her offhand pessimistic comments were affecting her daughter's attitudes. "My friends say I bring them down," sobbed Julie. "They say that I always put down their ideas and say they won't work so they might as well save their energy." Erin heard her own words in what her daughter was sharing. Over time she had to learn to change what she said about the future in order to provide an adequate model for her daughter.

Being aware of the effects of our prophecies can help us to model the positive. It is not just a sentimental superstition that positive thinking affects what happens to us. What we foretell actually can construct the future because it creates our mental attitudes and expectations. Even if things don't turn out the way we want, thinking the best can only make us more resilient.

Most of us go through life relatively unaware of the effects of modeling. If we can be alert to them, we might alter what we tend to say or do in front of children. The point, however, is to accept the power of modeling without feeling guilty, and to learn to use it to advantage. Once conscious of the fact that what adults say programs children, one can try to create positive programs.

In future chapters, when discussing specific areas of life such as learning or handling fears, this book will describe the way modeling self-talk can be used to help children meet challenges more fully.

STEP 5: SUBSTITUTING GOOD TALK FOR BAD

Now that you have become aware of your own role in creating a child's self-talk, you may be ready for experimenting with your child to change some of the ways he talks to himself. In subsequent chapters, you will become more expert at using modeling for that purpose. But this step gives you the principles through which you can help a child learn to help himself.

Since you have already introduced the idea of self-talk and its effects, you can suggest to the child that it's fun to experiment with changing self-talk to be able to do what she wants in life. You might want to use the analogy of a computer and how it can be programmed to perform certain tasks.

You can use the example of Olympic medalists and how they use positive self-talk to enable them to perform in new and more rigorous ways. The technique can allow people to do things they never thought they were capable of. In the following sections you will learn the three basic approaches to creating more positive self-talk: using positive affirmations, using cue words, and talking back to negative voices.

POSITIVE AFFIRMATIONS

Positive affirmations are one of the most powerful programs we can use to change our thinking, our reactions, and our images of ourselves.

Affirmations describe our inner state or outer reality the way we would like it to be. They give us a head start in reaching our goals because they help us see ourselves having already attained the goal. Affirmations work because the brain actually begins to give signals to the body to react as if that reality already exists.

An affirmation is usually stated as a simple message like, "My mind is calm and steady." Saying those words when we are in a receptive state helps to create calmness and steadiness. The more we repeat the affirmation, and the more open to it we are, the more powerful it becomes. The words themselves act like a signal in the brain and the body changes its chemical reactions to become calm and peaceful.

The most important things about affirmations are that they

- reflect the *child's* goals for herself, not yours;
- use the *child's* words, not yours;
- be worded positively (e.g., "I am calm and steady," not "I won't panic").

Your role with affirmations is that of facilitator. You can explain how affirmations work and perhaps share some affirmations you have used or might use in the future. If the child is interested in seeing how affirmations work, begin by having her explore some goals she would like to accomplish: for example, not getting nervous before a test, being able to remember information better when studying, or becoming a better soccer player.

Then you can help her to state these goals as if they have already been accomplished. Help her to put them in her own words.

"I am always calm and in control before a test."
"I've got the best memory around."
"I am turning into the kind of soccer player I want to be."

You can start by having a child practice affirmations before bed or at a quiet time at home. An older child can practice on her own and report the results. Ask her how affirmations affect her thoughts and feelings at the time. You can explain to your child that affirmations take time to work. It is best to repeat them four or five times every day. Bedtime seems a good time, since the mind is more relaxed and open to suggestion. She shouldn't look for instant results, but you might talk every few days to see how she thinks her affirmations are helping her. She should look for effects in herself—her own inner feelings of strength, calm, and control in the situation—not in external events or the behavior of others around her.

As a child tries out affirmations, she may get a sense that she wants to change them or elaborate on them.

> "It is easy for me to do well at basketball. I can move around the court and score baskets with ease."
> "My mind is open when I'm studying. I can remember all the information I need."
> "It is easy for me to make friends. I can talk to people easily and feel comfortable and relaxed."

Once a child or adolescent practices using affirmations during quiet times at home, he can try using them at the times he needs them outside the house.

For example, before a test a child might say something like, "My mind is calm and steady. I can easily find the answers I am looking for." Before a game she might say, "It's natural to be nervous. Everyone gets nervous. My body will react the way I want it to."

USING CUE WORDS

Over time, a child can learn to reduce an affirmation to just a few words. A powerful tool for inducing relaxation is using cue words or phrases in problematic settings. A cue word or phrase simply summarizes and represents a certain state or condition. The word must have a special meaning for that person.

Psychiatrist David Soskis of the University of Pennsylvania gives the example of an outstanding runner who came to him for help in overcoming "the wall" (an overwhelming sense of fatigue and physical resistance that overtakes most runners about three-quarters of the way through a marathon).

The runner had become so tense anticipating the wall that he was even beginning to run poorly at the start of races. He came up with the words *strong and steady*, the way he wanted to feel in the situation. He used these words after relaxing and before starting a race.

These cue words helped him to feel much stronger and steadier in his running because he was *telling* himself that he would feel that way. *And* they actually helped him improve his performance.

TALKING BACK TO NEGATIVE VOICES

When you first observed your child's self-talk, you probably noticed negative remarks she made about herself, her abilities, challenges in her life, or other people. Since negative assertions tend to dilute energy and confidence and keep people from doing their best, they must be opposed.

The best way to combat negative voices is to make a child aware of their effects. Most children are in the habit of saying so many negative things about themselves and others, either seriously or in teasing, that they have no idea their statements have an effect on them. Criticizing children for negative talk will only make them resist efforts to help. However, when they seem receptive you can ask them questions that help them become alert to the possible consequences of what they say:

"Have you ever noticed that telling yourself how unfair someone else is makes it even harder to hold in your anger?"

"Have you ever thought about how saying 'I can't' makes you feel helpless? That's how it makes me feel."

Once a child seems open to the idea that negative self-talk might affect him adversely, you can give him concrete ways to challenge those voices. A challenge is a statement that questions the reality of what the negative voice is saying. Challenges diminish the power of negative voices by countering them with realistic and positive responses.

When your daughter mentions a problem she feels negatively about, or when she has been involved in a negative situation, you can respond with the idea of challenging—aloud or internally—a negative voice. You might say, "Whenever I sit down to study for my class, a voice inside of me says, 'You don't know what you're doing. What makes you feel you can learn that stuff?' I hate that voice. It makes me feel stupid. But I've learned to challenge what it says and then it goes away. I tell myself I'm a good learner. I do well on my tests and I can learn whatever I want."

You can help children better if you understand that negative voices gain power by filtering out the positive and making things absolute. Rather than saying, "This may be a difficult test, so you'll have to study harder than usual," the negative voice says, "You're going to fail. There's no use trying. You always fail at science. It's humiliating to try your best and still fail, so why try at all?"

Children need to understand that negative voices tend to be absolute and they need concrete suggestions for challenging them effectively. Here are some examples:

Negative voice:

"You're no good at spelling. You have to look up every single word in the dictionary to see how it's spelled."

Challenge:

"Having to try hard and spend time on something doesn't mean I'm not good at it. People who do great things try really hard, too. Besides, some of the best writers around have trouble with spelling."

Negative voice:

"Sally doesn't want to play with you. That means she doesn't like you anymore. Nobody likes you."

Challenge:

"Just because Sally doesn't want to play with me right now doesn't mean she doesn't like me. It certainly doesn't mean that nobody likes me. We all like to play with different people sometimes."

Negative voice:

"This test is going to be a catastrophe. You know you're not good at tests. You get too nervous."

Challenge:

"Sometimes I do really well on tests. I don't have to get nervous if I tell myself that I'm steady and calm."

Negative voice:

"Look how stupid you are, you made a mistake."

Challenge:

"Mistakes aren't bad. That's how people learn."

Using affirmations and learning to recognize and challenge negative self-talk are important ways of shaping self-talk to fit our needs and the demands of the situation. By helping a child be aware of what he says to himself, and the effects of that talk, you can help him see how he can talk to himself in new ways. He can learn the power of positive self-talk to change his inner state at any moment. The purpose of this step isn't to abolish negative voices, because that isn't really possible. But anyone can learn to strengthen the power of positive voices and counteract the power of negative thoughts and assertions.

These five steps are the basis of learning about and shaping a child's self-talk. After reading them, you should have a picture of the process of tuning in to self-talk and making it more positive.

One crucial point has been omitted in these steps, however. What we have described is an ongoing process, not something that you do once or twice and then see dramatic results. Working on self-talk is a lifetime proposition requiring patience and constant reinforcement. It is crucial to encourage children in their efforts to talk to themselves positively and to reinforce their openness to do so through praise and support.

These five steps will be referred to again and again throughout this book. In the next chapter we will talk about specialized techniques for changing self-talk. If you are willing to work at these techniques with your child, we think you will find them to be powerful allies in building confidence, self-reliance, and a mature sense of self and worth. But they do take work. Children shouldn't be promised instant results or magic. Changing self-talk actually programs the mind in new ways, and that takes time and patience. More and more people are agreeing that the results are definitely worth the effort.

· 3 ·
ADVANCED TECHNIQUES FOR CHANGING SELF-TALK

• • •

Self-talk is even more effective when it involves visualization. The combination of the words and images somehow allows the child to use more of his mental powers to focus his attention. This chapter presents six techniques—*relaxation, remembering past successes, mental rehearsal, inoculation, problem solving,* and *talking to the wizard*—all of which combine self-talk with imagery. These techniques expand on the five steps described in Chapter 2, and are designed to help children with specific problems such as irrational fear, learning and school problems, making friends, and so on. Not all six of these techniques are equally effective and appropriate in every situation, but they give you a broad range of approaches and tools to use in helping your child become more confident and secure.

RELAXATION

Thinking about a child sprawled in front of the TV or playing a game with a friend, you may wonder why teaching relaxation is necessary. But we often confuse recreation with relaxation. Recreation is both positive and important, but it is not the same as systematically letting go of muscular tension so that deeper and deeper levels of relaxation are attained.

You also may wonder why children today need such techniques when kids in the past seemed to get along fine without them. The fact is that today life is much more hectic than it once was, and the modern child needs to cope with stresses previous generations never dreamed of. The cumulative effects of external pressures and negative self-talk often lead to muscle tension and strong negative emotions such as fear, anxiety, grief, or anger. For example, a child who tells himself that he has to be popular but that no one wants to play with him will become anxious when the bell rings to announce recess. If he gives himself many negative messages throughout the day and experiences demands he thinks he cannot meet, his anxiety will be chronic; he will be unable to relax.

We know that challenging negative self-talk is one way to control intense negative emotions. But we also know that when someone is really upset, he is not receptive to input or change. His mind shuts down and he is controlled by emotions rather than *in* control of them. If you've ever had someone trying to "talk sense into you" when you were really upset, you know how gripping strong emotions can be. Just as you need to get hold of yourself before you can listen to what someone else is telling you, so you need to relax or calm down before you can listen to your *own* rational statements.

There are many relaxation techniques that are effective with children. They range from simple to complex. On the simple end of the continuum is teaching the child how to *breathe deeply* and exhale slowly, usually to the count of three, four, or five. Deep breathing has the advantage over more complex methods in that it can be done unobtrusively anywhere, anytime—for example, before answering a difficult question ("Why are you late?"), before asking someone for something you don't think they'll give you ("Can I play with you?"), in the middle of taking a test or engaging in any stressful activity, and *after* the activity is over, as a means of regaining a relaxed, steady state.

This is how you might explain the relaxation technique to your child:

"I want you to breathe in to the count of five. Be sure to take in as much air as you possibly can." Demonstrate, pointing out how your diaphragm (not your chest, but your midriff) expands when you take a deep breath. Say, "Now, when I nod, I want you to exhale slowly as I say 'R-E-L-A-X' to the count of five. Say 'relax' to yourself, also, as I say it."

Explain to the child that whenever he begins to feel anxious or tense, he can take a deep breath like this and exhale it slowly as he says "relax" to himself. Since it is physiologically impossible to exhale slowly and be tense at the same time, he will effectively be pairing the word *relax* with physical relaxation. Just as Pavlov taught his dogs to salivate at the sound of a bell that had previously been rung whenever he gave them food, the child will be teaching himself to relax just by saying the word *relax* to himself.

Another popular relaxation technique for adults is *autogenic training*. Children can learn a simplified version of it. Demonstrate first and then have the child follow these steps:

1. Sit in an armchair or lie on the floor in a comfortable position with all body parts supported.
2. Close your eyes and repeat each phrase slowly, taking about five seconds. Pause about three seconds before repeating the phrase. Repeat each phrase four times before moving on to the next one.

    "My right arm is heavy" (you can substitute "warm" for "heavy" if you prefer).
    "My left arm is heavy."
    "Both my arms are heavy."
    "My right leg is heavy."
    "My left leg is heavy."
    "Both my legs are heavy."
    "My arms and legs are heavy."

3. Before stopping, say to yourself, "When I open my eyes, I will feel refreshed and alert." Breathe a few deep breaths and stretch your limbs before you continue your regular activities.

After the child has practiced this technique several times a day for a week or more, he can begin to intersperse some of the following messages:

"I feel quiet inside."
"My whole body is quiet, comfortable, and relaxed."
"My mind is quiet."
"I can withdraw my thoughts from the world, go inside, and be totally at peace."

This technique can be even further simplified for young children by just teaching them to close their eyes, take a few deep breaths, and repeat to themselves a message similar to those above to help calm themselves.

Before teaching a fairly complex strategy like autogenic training, you should ask the child if he already has a way of relaxing that works well for him. Many children (as well as adults) use *imagery* to relax. They get comfortable, close their eyes for a few minutes, and visualize a favorite scene. Often it's a mountain or ocean view. Sometimes school-aged children think of secret forts or tree houses. Sometimes with small children, scenes involving a parent (for example, being tucked in, read to, or rocked) can be comforting. Or they might get an image of a favorite holiday, like Christmas, with everyone gathered around singing or eating. It might even be thoughts of a favorite stuffed animal or imaginary playmate. The point is that relaxing images are very individual. A mental image that helps one person relax may actually make another person tense.

If the child does have an image she uses to relax, you'd be better off building on it than teaching a whole new technique. Once you've discovered what the image is, experiment with the child to see if it can be used more effectively. If you're successful, you can write out what you both came up with and make a tape for her to use for several weeks. The tape could be made in your voice or your child's. After listening to the tape once or twice a day for two to three weeks, she may be able to just close her eyes anytime she begins to worry or feel anxious, summon the image in her mind, and get herself relaxed.

There are also commercially made tapes available to help children relax. "Self-Image for Children" (part of *The Love Tapes* series by Effective Learning Systems) is an example.

REMEMBERING PAST SUCCESSES

Being able to call up the memory of past successes is a powerful tool for learning to talk to oneself positively and meet challenges successfully. Adults play a crucial role in helping children to master this skill.

Imagine these scenarios:

Situation 1:

An eleven-year-old boy comes home from school and throws his books on the table. "I'm really nervous about my math test. I know I'm going to fail. I get so nervous during tests that I can't think straight. My hands start sweating and my heart starts beating fast and I can't even do the problems."

Mother: "It's because you don't study enough. If you studied instead of watching TV you wouldn't be nervous. You would know the answers and you wouldn't have to worry."

Situation 2:

The boy comes home and confesses his pre-test jitters. Instead of criticizing him for negative traits, which may or may not be relevant, his mother tries hard to think of a time when he has experienced real success at an academic undertaking.

Mother: "Remember the time you got an A on your math test? I remember how proud you felt. I remember you said it had been a really hard test but you had been able to get every problem done on time. Can you remember how you felt during that test? How would you describe those feelings? Why don't you close your eyes and go back to that time? See if you can recapture that feeling of calm and confidence. Can you remember how that felt?"

Remembering past successes can be done without trying to visualize the past event or reexperience the feeling, but when the child does use visualization, the experience is much more powerful.

Psychologists have found that recalling past successes is an effective tool for reestablishing belief in ourselves. Once a child has reestablished this belief in himself, he should have added motivation to tackle the situation and do whatever is necessary to succeed. Thus, the boy whose mother never even mentioned that he needed to study will probably study harder and more effectively than the boy whose mother told him to study. Recalling his past successes has changed his perspective about his chances of succeeding. In other words, he's more likely to study because he now believes it will make a difference.

Even if you know from personal experience how powerful a tool recalling past successes is, the child may not immediately see its usefulness. Nor will he be able to do it without your help. The six-year-old can't remember what he achieved at age four and the fourteen-year-old may not care.

A child or young person can appreciate the usefulness of systematically remembering past successes only if she is patient enough to try experimenting with these memories. She has to experience the boost in performance level that recalling and talking about those accomplishments can give her.

If you present this technique carefully, following each step provided below, the child will experience that boost.

1. Try to remember a success that provided the emotional tone the child needs now. For example, a child who feels she can't learn something needs to recall a time when she felt the exhilaration of mastering something new. A young person who is nervous before a test or sports event needs

to remember an occasion when he excelled at such an event. If these past experiences included initial nervousness that was overcome, so much the better. She can remember how nervous she felt and how much control she was able to exert over that nervousness. That was part of the success.

2. Remind the child of the success. "I remember the time you were scared to go to swim-team practice and you ended up being swimmer of the day."

    If you can't remember such an experience, you can ask the child or young person to recall a time when he had a sense of real success. Sometimes neither of you can think of a past triumph that is similar enough to the present situation to have credibility with the child. (For instance, he may discount the success he felt when he learned to ride a bike because the task was so different from learning long division.) If this happens, an almost as effective technique is to have the child picture one of his heroes in the scene and try to feel what that hero would feel. The hero might be a peer, a TV or rock star, a relative, or almost anyone; it doesn't matter. The important thing is that the child sees this person as competent and self-assured in this particular area.

3. Help the child reexperience the feelings he had during that earlier achievement. He will be most receptive to this kind of reprogramming if he's in a relaxed state. So, depending on the age of the child, either help him get relaxed or suggest he relax himself. Then you might ask, "Can you remember how you felt that day?" It is important to get the child to talk about the experience so that he recalls it as vividly as possible. You want him to call up a sensory-rich vision of his success—the people,

places colors, and feelings that he associates with the event.

You can enhance this effort by helping the child make his imagery more intense. Ask him to picture himself in the situation in vivid color, to make the image larger, and to step into or merge with the image of himself rather than viewing it from a separated or outside perspective. You can suggest that he re-create the scene and try to remember the textures, sights, sounds, and smells.

As he talks about the event, ask, "Can you feel now what you did then? Can you feel on top of the world and successful? Can you feel yourself sitting up straight, head erect, shoulders back?" The more intensely the child can recapture those feelings, the more this exercise can help him.

4. Once he has reexperienced these feelings, provide (or suggest that he provide for himself) the posthypnotic suggestion of being able to do it again. You might say, "Just as you passed a hard math test before, you can do it again." Since the achievement or success won't always be the same, he will often have to adapt it: "If I learned how to ride a bike, I can learn to ride a skateboard."

Saying these things to himself will provide verbal cues that he can use in the future. If he repeats these phrases to himself while he is picturing the success, he will begin to create a program. The feelings he is experiencing will begin to be associated with the positive statement about what he can do now.

Although this discusson of recalling past successes has focused primarily on *external* succcesses such as learning a new skill or performing well, some of the most important "wins" children need to acknowledge and recall are internal: the success of not losing one's temper; the success of enduring a fear and still going on; the success of overlooking a slight by a friend; the success of trying to feel positive even when one is down.

One of the ways you can help children recognize those attainments is by talking about your own struggles with internal issues and the progress you've made. You may not have thought about how valuable the technique is, but you may already do it instinctively.

Remembering past successes is an effective way to use the past to help overcome current challenges. The next technique focuses on the future to achieve the same goal.

MENTAL REHEARSAL

Mental rehearsal involves imagining as vividly as possible how one would look, feel, think, and act while performing a given task well or while controlling a strong emotion such as fear or anger.

To teach a child how to use mental rehearsal, follow these steps:

1. Introduce it by telling her you'd like to try an experiment to help her with her problem. Tell her that you will be helping her get an image of the way she wants to act and feel and that this technique has been found to be successful in assisting people to achieve all kinds of things—from overcoming shyness to winning Olympic gold medals.
2. Have her sit comfortably in a soft chair or on a couch. Turn the lights low and have the room as quiet as possible (no other people around, no TV, radio, or stereo).

3. Have her relax or help her relax, using whatever techniques work for her (deep breathing, imagining a relaxing scene, and so on).
4. Have her close her eyes and picture herself doing something; she should imagine looking, acting, and feeling the way she wants to look, act, and feel. Describe the scene thoroughly. You might close your eyes, too, so you can be sure that you are giving a complete description.

   For example: "You're sitting in class and the teacher starts to pass out the math test. You begin to feel yourself getting a little nervous so you take a deep breath and let it out slowly. You notice yourself getting calm again as you exhale, and you remind yourself that you studied hard for this test and that you are well prepared. Notice how you are able to maintain your confidence and clearheadedness even as you look at the test now in front of you."
5. Instruct her to "run the movie" herself for a while, and ask her tell you what's happening. If she starts to visualize herself in her old problem way, take over the directing again and see if you can help her recapture the positive image.
6. Do the exercise for only three to five minutes, but suggest that the child close her eyes and visualize herself in this way whenever she can throughout the day, and especially right before she goes to bed at night and gets up in the morning.

If a child has difficulty getting a vivid mental picture, have him visualize a time when he *did* act, think, and feel as he wants to now (recalling past successes). Once he reexperiences the confidence and sense of mastery he had then, he can mentally transfer those same feelings and actions to the new situation, visualizing it as vividly as he just did with his past success image.

Mental rehearsal is a powerful tool for controlling negative emotions such as fear and anger. It is also an effective way to improve a wide range of skills, including, but not limited to, social skills, athletic and physical skills, and academic skills. In fact, the only situation in which it might not be effective is a case where the child simply can't, for whatever reasons, imagine or visualize vividly. Children for whom this is true can mentally rehearse what they will say to themselves and others in a difficult situation. Such rehearsal is often helpful, but it lacks the power of visualizing.

Mental rehearsal takes some practice, and it can't be done on the spot, that is, in the midst of the situation in which one wants to respond differently, but it is probably one of the most powerful mental techniques known today.

INOCULATION

Unlike mental rehearsal, which is most effective when practiced in a totally relaxed state, far away in space and time from whatever causes the child a problem, stress inoculation is specifically designed to help reduce anger or fear just *before* they occur. Just as a polio shot inoculates a child against getting the disease in the future, stress-inoculation practice protects the child from having a stress reaction (anger or fear) in the future. You can rehearse this process with the child so that he can use it with himself before or during a stressful situation. Once he's learned this skill, he'll be more able to confront and handle situations that previously caused him to get anxious or angry.

Stress inoculation has four phases or steps. When put together in this particular sequence, these steps have been shown to be especially effective in reducing fear and anger in adults as well as children. The phases of stress inoculation are as follows:

Phase 1: *preparing for the stressful event*

Before the child is in the situation that he thinks will make him angry or afraid, he takes time to make positive self-statements and to imagine himself being successful. He might say, "What do I have to do? Let's figure out a plan to deal with this. I can handle it. There's no need to worry. I need to take a few deep breaths, get relaxed, and picture how I'll handle this."

Phase 2: *confronting and handling the problem*

As he enters the situation, the child continues to talk to himself, saying something like, "Stay calm. Just continue to relax. One step at a time, I can handle it." In thinking about his anger he might say, "Don't take it personally," or "Don't get all bent out of shape. I don't have to prove myself. There's no point in getting angry. For a person to be this irritable, he must be awfully unhappy."

Phase 3: *coping with anger or fear*

If the situation progresses and the child's emotions escalate, he continues to talk to himself. If his anger (or fear) keeps rising, he might say to himself, "My muscles are starting to feel tight. Time to relax and slow down. Take a deep breath and imagine the tension leaving my body. This anger is a signal of what I need to do. Time to talk to myself. Try to cooperate. Maybe we're both right. Just because he's making a fool of himself doesn't mean I have to."

Phase 4: self-reward

As the child successfully talks to himself and keeps his anger or fear in check, he needs to praise himself. Statements he might make could include, "I did it! It's getting better each time I use this stuff. Give myself a pat on the back. It wasn't as bad as I expected. It wasn't really anything to get upset about."

A child might enjoy rehearsing this procedure with you before a worrisome upcoming event. You could walk through it first, role-playing his part and talking to yourself out loud. Then he could try it, talking out loud as you play the other part. He should continue to practice until he can talk to himself silently at each phase. It is also important that he use his own words and phrases rather than just copying what you have said.

PROBLEM SOLVING

There are several problem-solving strategies that are commonly used with children, but the essential ingredients of each are to get the child to

1. define the problem,
2. consider options or choices,
3. look at the possible consequences of each option.

Many children act and *then* think—or worse, don't think at all. Young children, because of their limited capacity to think through a problem, tend to strike out when their needs are thwarted. Grabbing toys, pushing, pulling, and hitting are common behaviors among preschool children. As these children mature, they will begin to think of other, nonaggressive options to get what they want—especially if the adults in their lives ask them questions like, "What will happen if you take John's wagon? How will he feel? What might he do? How else could you handle the situation?"

If a child isn't experiencing negative consequences from his behavior, he may not see that there is a problem. Either you can *provide* negative consequences so the child perceives the problem or you can help him think about what *might* happen if he keeps acting that way. For example, an aggressive preschooler whose peers don't hit back may not respond to scoldings or even time-outs. Even if they were effective, neither of those options teaches him what to do *instead* of hitting. But asking him what will happen if he keeps hitting people may help him see that his friends might stop playing with him, stop liking him, or, eventually, even start hitting him back if he doesn't mend his ways. If you then ask, "What else could you do when you get angry?" the child will gradually learn other, more appropriate ways of getting what he wants.

Aggression is not the only problem that can be alleviated by teaching a child to consider alternatives and possible consequences. Any nonproductive emotional or behavioral pattern can be broken by practicing problem solving. For example, a child who is shy and tends to avoid talking to peers on the playground, but who wants friends, might ask herself, "What could I do instead of going off by myself at recess that might help me make friends?" As she considers possibilities, she will automatically project possible consequences and will reject some because they seem too scary, but if she keeps thinking about ways to start to get to know other people, she is bound to come up with one that doesn't feel like too big a risk. For instance, she might reject the idea of asking to join the kickball game because she just couldn't imagine speaking up like that in front of so many people. She might, however, feel comfortable with the option of looking for another girl on the playground who was by herself and asking if she wanted to play hopscotch.

TALKING TO THE WIZARD

Sometimes a child *knows* how to solve problems and challenge his negative self-talk, but in the heat of the moment he doesn't apply that knowledge. The wise, rational part of him (the wizard) seems to be better at dealing with *other* people's problems than his own. But he can use this truth to advantage by pretending it is, in fact, a friend who has the problem, not he.

Let's use the example of a ten-year-old boy, James, who comes flying through the front door and starts raving to his mother about how he's "gonna kill" the neighbor boy who "never" does what James wants him to do and who "always has to be the boss," and so on.

When a child is that upset, you can't help him get in touch with his wizard until you understand what happened. As James's mother listened, she asked questions and finally gleaned that the other boy hadn't wanted to play a certain computer game but had gone along with it at James's insistence. He apparently got bored after a short time and just shut off the game and walked out of the room, leaving James alone in front of a blank screen.

James's mother didn't tell him how irrational he was and that the neighbor didn't "always" get his own way. Instead, she let James cool down a little and reflected his feelings back to him, saying, "I can see how upset you are, James. You're not only mad, your feelings are hurt, too, because Myles just left you there." After a bit, she tentatively said, "You know, I overheard you give Joseph advice the other day when he was upset like this. Why don't you see if you can kind of step back from being so upset and ask yourself, 'What would I tell Joseph if he came in and told me what I just told Mom?' "

Children can draw upon any positive model they have for a wizard. In teaching a child how to use mental rehearsal, for instance, you might find that he can't even *imagine* himself speaking confidently, hitting a home run, or whatever. He may not even be able to think of a past success and apply it to the current situation. But, if this happens, he will probably be able to tell you who *could* talk confidently or hit a home run. That model (or wizard) might be a classmate, an older sibling, a TV or movie star, or a well-known athlete.

If you can get the child to imagine how that model would handle the situation, he can use that information to guide his own thoughts, feelings, and behavior. For example, you might ask, "How would so-and-so introduce himself to a girl?" or "How would that math whiz in your class, Tony, study for a test? What would he say to himself when he was studying?"

CONCLUSION

This chapter presents six advanced techniques—relaxation, remembering past successes, mental rehearsal, inoculation, problem solving, and talking to the wizard. By combining self-talk with imagery, these approaches help a child utilize both his logical, rational abilities and his creative, intuitive side. They are more powerful than methods that make use of left-brain functions only, but most are also more complicated. Because of this, they may not be appropriate for children under seven.

Consider these strategies adjuncts to the five steps presented in Chapter 2. Experiment with them; have fun with them, but don't force them on an unwilling youngster. A child who begins to experience the power of positive self-talk will eventually want to expand his ability to focus his attention. When he reaches that point, he will be motivated to learn and master some of these advanced and extremely powerful techniques.

· 4 ·
KEEPING ANGER UNDER CONTROL

USING SELF-TALK TO GAIN SELF-CONTROL

■ ■ ■

I used to throw temper tantrums as a kid. One time I threw myself down on a hardwood floor and flailed about so wildly that I hurt myself. My parents told me what a bad temper I had and how I needed to control it. That made me even angrier since I didn't know how to control it.

We relive angry feelings when we see anger in our children, which can make helping them difficult. If we ourselves didn't learn effective ways to deal with anger when we were children, it's especially challenging to teach our children to deal with it. In fact, many adults don't know how to control their tempers. When their children get angry it often makes them angry too. Having a child with a temper that is out of control can make one feel guilty and inadequate.

Anger isn't wrong. It is actually a signal that can be helpful in pointing out internal or external conflicts or ways one needs to mobilize oneself. Anger can startle us into fleeing from a dangerous situation or give us the energy to defend ourselves.

Anger can let us know that there is something that needs to be straightened out with another person. It can give us the feedback that something is out of balance.

But when anger is one of the dominant ways an adult or a child reacts to life, that habit can cause serious problems. In the past people referred to this type of behavior as if it were a God-given flaw that couldn't be altered: "He has a bad temper"; "She had a short fuse"; "Be careful with him, he's explosive."

One theory has also related habitual anger to long-term health problems. For example, reacting consistently with anger is a part of Type A behavior—a cluster of characteristics associated with heart attacks and other stress-related illnesses.

But the inability to manage one's temper has many more short-range consequences. Children who can't control their angry outbursts are more frequently disciplined by teachers and rejected by their peers.

Today we know that the inability to control disruptive anger can be changed. And studies show that changing one's self-talk is one of the quickest and easiest ways to do that.

THE RELATIONSHIP BETWEEN SELF-TALK AND ANGER

Every child has to struggle if he is to learn to handle the expression of anger in socially acceptable ways. Although babies and toddlers express anger freely, as a child moves into the preschool years the adults around him typically try to help him find positive ways to deal with his upsets. This transforming of powerful emotions is one of the most challenging tasks of the preschool years. One method is to help the child develop an inner voice that can calm him and help him think of alternatives to physical aggression or yelling. Later, self-talk can help him empathize with the other person and be more objective about the situations involved. If children persist in problems with anger and aggression beyond the preschool years, it is often because they haven't developed that positive inner voice.

The inner voice is self-instructive but it can often be heard out loud. One four-year-old used to repeat an admonition to himself when he felt particularly aggressive: "I will not hit my friends. I will not hit my friends." Later those words were assimilated into his inner speech.

Aggressive children may have a dual problem related to self-talk: First, they haven't developed a voice capable of calming them; second, they may have an inflaming voice that actually incites them to more anger.

Picture this typical childhood scene: John is playing intramural basketball. He is standing directly under the basket and yells to a teammate to pass the ball to him. Instead, the teammate tries to make the basket himself, he misses, and the other team gets the ball. John says to himself, "He just didn't want to pass to me. He never gives me the ball and now he's probably lost us the game. No one ever gives me a chance." In a fury, he runs across the court and knocks down his teammate.

Now picture this same scene: John under the basket telling his teammate to pass him the ball, the teammate shooting and missing, and the other team stealing the ball. But this time John doesn't inflame himself with negative self-talk. Internally he says, "That's the third time he has done that this season. He must be trying to make points, but it's messing up the team. I think we should bring it up with the coach."

In each case, the external situation was the same. What changed was John's interpretation and self-talk. In the first scene, John stoked his anger by telling himself his teammate's actions were directed at him personally and were causing his team to lose. Through self-talk, John's emotions went from irritation to anger.

In the second scene, self-talk helped John to manage his emotions, see the situation objectively, take a problem-solving approach.

Most people, even adults, don't act with this much maturity all the time. It's easy to get caught up in interpreting events in ways that inflame, or undermine self-control.

But reacting to an isolated event isn't the only way that self-talk plays a crucial role in anger. Nagging resentments, ongoing feuds, and even irritability are all kept alive at least in part by internal speech.

When people aren't helped to work through their angry feelings, the feelings often go underground and resentments can build. At forty-five, Mary had a long-standing problem with her mother. She resented her mother's continual interference and smothering behavior. One thing that prevented Mary from talking to her mother about the situation was the way she framed the relationship in her mind through her inner speech. Mary was convinced, and told herself daily, that her mother couldn't change and the problems in their relationship were destined to continue. This self-talk perpetuated Mary's feelings of helplessness and irritation. Everyone has heard stories of people like Mary who have spent years angry at a parent, or resentful of a sibling. It is possible that those feelings have been kept alive by self-talk that prevented them from seeking solutions to the problem.

PHASES OF DEVELOPMENT

At certain stages of development, children are more prone to anger or tantrums than at other stages. Periods of equilibrium are followed by periods of disequilibrium. But if children have been helped to deal with them, those problems often dissipate as the young people pass into the next phase of development.

However, often when problems such as angry outbursts or irritability appear to have subsided or dissipated, they resurface at another stage in a slightly different form.

There seems to be a sensitive period in childhood for developing self-talk. That stage is during the preschool years. If positive self-talk is not established, problems with anger may persist and cause children ongoing social or personal problems.

It isn't clear exactly why some children develop this crucial form of self-talk at an appropriate age while others do not. But it is known that teaching children to talk to themselves positively at any age can mediate recurring problems and help them develop self-control.

During the preschool years children are just learning to be aware of their feelings and beginning to give them labels. They need to be taught and reminded again and again to put feelings into words rather than acting out impulsively. They can be coached to say what bothers them even after they have been involved in an altercation, so that they can carry that learning to the next incident.

In the early elementary years, children continue to learn how to express angry feelings while avoiding physical aggression. They can also begin to solve problems of interaction, and start to plan ahead in order to avoid angry feelings in the future.

Older children can put themselves in someone else's shoes and even role-play situations. They often need help and reminders about how put-downs can hurt other people, or how bad it feels to be left out.

HANDLING ANGER THROUGH SELF-TALK

SHARING YOUR EXPERIENCES

One of the most effective ways to help children with self-talk is to tell them how you handle problems with anger.

You might say, "When someone makes me angry at the office, I often have to tell myself that they are probably having an off day. If I start to think that they are trying to get to me, then I'm likely to overreact and start arguing with them. Then everything goes downhill because everyone's unhappy."

This can be done with a group as well as individually. One kindergarten teacher wanted to work on problems with anger in her class. During her morning circle time she told the children she had a problem. She said that that morning something had happened at home and she had become really angry. She said that afterward she felt angry at herself and really bad. She asked the class for solutions. She asked them what she could say to herself to prevent getting that angry in the future and to stop feeling awful about herself.

Children love to hear about what you did when you were their age. Use your present consciousness of self-talk and project back to your childhood. Try to remember how you kept yourself from striking back when a friend offended you or how you tried to manage your temper with your parents or siblings. You might be able to make up some scripts describing what you said to yourself that would be instructive and helpful.

LOOK AT YOUR DISCIPLINE

One of the primary ways children learn to talk to themselves in angry ways is through the discipline adults use with them. *Discipline is one of the most powerful ways to model self-talk about anger.* Studies show that children who have trouble controlling their aggression often have parents who are physically and verbally aggressive with them.

Realizing that what you say in a discipline situation has an effect on a child's self-talk can help you understand his angry feelings. Compare these two remarks:

"Stop that or you are going to get it."
"If you jump on the couch, the springs will break. If you want to jump, please do it outside."

The first example is a trigger for anger. Whether a parent says that to a child or a child repeats it to himself in another situation when someone is doing something he doesn't like, the response it will evoke is anger. In the second case, the rational explanation reassures and calms; it allows the child to develop a picture of how he can react to situations in rational ways.

When adults speak to children in threatening ways, children learn to speak to others in the same way. For example, threatening to hit a child may or may not stop the aggressive behavior, but it will prompt the child to tell himself in similar situations that he has the right to hit someone.

Trying to talk to children rationally during emotionally charged situations may seem like an indirect route to helping them control their behavior, but it's not. You can even make children aware of your internal processes by saying, "Now, I'm reminding myself not to talk to myself crossly so that it won't come out that way when we talk to each other now."

PINPOINTING ANGRY SITUATIONS

Once you are aware of how you may be contributing to angry self-talk and the feelings that come out of it, you can start to observe the child and the issues that seem to inflame him. What situations make him angry? Here are some examples of common problems and the self-talk associated with them.

Boundary problems with siblings or friends

All children experience upsets over people taking their possessions or invading their space. But if this is a constant issue that makes playing with other children difficult, you need to focus on the attitudes the child brings to the situation.

Persistent problems with boundaries often come up when a child thinks that other people *should* do as she wants or that she *should* have her own way. She tells herself internally that other people are mean if they don't comply with her wishes, or that they don't like her. Aloud she might say, "That's mine," or "You're not being fair."

These are also developmental issues. For preschoolers and kindergartners, boundary problems are common because children are just learning to respect other points of view. Still, some children tend to react more persistently or violently to apparent infringements on their territory or with their things. A child who carries this tendency into the preschool years needs to develop another form of self-talk; he needs to tell himself that sharing and cooperation are important and that his ability to share and take turns are signs that he's growing up. He needs to be able to remind himself that he doesn't *have* to have his own way and that when someone else refuses to do what he wants it doesn't mean that person doesn't like him.

Communication problems with siblings or friends

Some communication problems are an inevitable part of growing up. But if a child's feelings are constantly getting hurt, or if frustrations about communication bring more pain than pleasure to her friendships, than she needs help. These problems are sometimes associated with self-talk that makes her feel other people *should* be considerate of her or know what she is thinking. Communication problems can also be related to two other ideas that permeate self-talk: 1) that she can't say anything negative or people won't like her and, 2) that it's essential to have everyone's approval. Out loud, she might say, "People won't like me if I say that," or "If I do that they won't like me."

Resistance to discipline or authority

Most children have some resistance to discipline, but when a child's anger over discipline makes working with him a constant battle, it's time to focus on his attitudes. These problems are often related to self-talk that makes him feel life is unfair or that he *should* be able to do what he wants. They may also be related to the idea that he has to stand up for himself or people will push him around. Out loud, he might say, "You can't tell me what to do," or I don't have to," or "That's not fair."

ASK CHILDREN TO TALK ABOUT SITUATIONS THAT MAKE THEM ANGRY

The usual ways of talking with children about angry situations make them defensive: "Why did you do that?" "Why are you talking in that tone?" These approaches project the idea that anger isn't okay and they should hide those feelings. However, if they are ever going to learn to get angry feelings under some control, they have to become *more* aware of them and of what triggers them. If children are going to monitor the expression of their anger, they have to begin by understanding what they say to themselves that makes them angrier. Then they can start to tell themselves different things to reduce the anger.

Your goal is not only to get information about his reactions, but also to make the child aware of how he's interpreting the situation. You want him to feel that there are different ways to view the same situation, and that what he tells himself about it influences the way he feels and reacts. You can't do this effectively by lecturing or preaching. You need to let him discover his own ideas and reactions for himself.

You can start by asking a child to describe a provocative situation. What happened to upset him? How would he have liked things to be? How would he change the situation so that he wouldn't have those feelings? You might ask a younger child, "If you had a magic wand, what would you do to make things different?" You could ask an older child, "If you had the power to change things, what would you do?"

Once you have established her version of the event, ask her to tell you what she said to herself during the situation. See if she'll describe what she said in order: what she said to herself first, and what she said next, as much as she can recall. If she can't remember, have her take a guess. Then ask, "How did what you said make you feel? When you said, 'That's not fair,' did it make you even madder at your friend?"

You can explain that the things we say to ourselves can make us angrier. You can say that it is natural to be afraid or angry sometimes, but that she can also learn to say things to herself that make her feel better rather than worse. Again, sharing an example from your own life is extremely helpful.

If there were other people involved in the situation, ask the child what she thinks they might have been saying to themselves, and how their self-talk might have affected them.

Ask a young child to draw a picture of the situation. Then you could write what he said to himself and make it into a story. An older child could make a cartoon or series of cartoons that would include his self-talk and the self-talk of others as captions.

USE HYPOTHETICAL SITUATIONS TO TALK ABOUT ANGER

Books provide wonderful opportunities to show another person's self-talk, but you can also use TV characters to elicit the same imaginative process.

Here is an example of a hypothetical situation that you might use with a child to elicit conversation about her self-talk:

Randa and Sara made arrangements to go to the movies together, but when Randa called on Saturday morning, Sara said she had made other plans. What do you think Randa said to herself? How do you think the things she said made her feel?

Make up other situations that you think a younger or older child would be interested in talking about.

Once you have discussed self-talk with the child, you can take the next step, which allows her to turn destructive self-talk into positive, reassuring inner dialogues that permit more self-control.

USE AFFIRMATIONS TO SHORT-CIRCUIT ANGER

Affirmations help create the desired reality. But what does that have to do with anger? When children find themselves in difficult situations where their emotions feel suddenly out of control, repeating an internal affirmation can help them to manage such encounters more easily.

Here are some affirmations that can help children control their anger.

"It's all right to feel angry, but I can tell other people how I feel rather than hurting them."
"It makes me strong inside if I ignore mean things that other people do."
"I don't have to let the things other people do make me angry. I have a choice about the way I respond."
"I'm the kind of person who can talk things out with other people and solve problems."

You might suggest that a child use affirmations like these or make up his own when he's on the verge of losing his temper. Repeating the affirmation to himself can give him strength. It also makes him pause rather than act impulsively. Studies show that most children who have problems with lashing out at others don't think about the consequences before they act. Affirmations also help children drown out negative voices. Using affirmations shouldn't, however, make a child feel that his original feelings are wrong, only that he has the ability to create new feelings and to help things turn out the way he wants. Experts sometimes suggest that a child repeat an affirmation to himself at least five times. The repetition helps him keep his equilibrium when he is being thrown off balance.

In addition to helping a child in a volatile situation, affirmations repeated at various times during the day can help a child remember that he is working on self-control. Children may like to know or be reminded that scientists have found that people can do incredible things by programming their conscious minds in just this way.

CHALLENGING THE ANGRY INNER VOICE

When you teach a child to challenge, you give him counterstatements that oppose the triggers for his anger. Challenges can lift us out of the raw emotions we are feeling and help us see things more rationally. Challenges give a child the sense that he has options about how he views and reacts to things. They should help him realize that he can solve problems satisfactorily.

Here are some examples of statements that challenge negative voices:

Negative voice:

"I can't handle this; I'm going to fall apart."

Challenge:

"I'm stronger than I think; it's the way we react to things that makes them harder."

Negative voice:

"He's deliberately trying to get me, and I'm going to get revenge."

Challenge:

"He probably didn't mean to hurt my feelings. Maybe we could talk about it. Telling people my feelings works better than getting angry."

To help a child make up challenges that will be effective for him, start by asking what he is already saying to himself. Then do a reality check: "Is that the way things *really* are?" or "Does that sound right?" This is less threatening than saying, "You're not thinking clearly." You want to invite the child to examine his own ideas and modify them himself.

The goal is to help the child see that what he is saying to himself is probably more absolute or one-sided than the reality. Once he sees this, he can develop a challenge that will help him to think more realistically.

GETTING FROM ANGER TO PROBLEM SOLVING

The self-talk of children who have a problem with anger or fear often keeps them from concrete problem solving. Negative self-talk can make anger so overwhelming that one can't think of anything constructive to do. Children who have ongoing problems with anger have often not learned to engage in internal problem solving. But you can teach them to solve problems when you discuss their self-talk with them.

For example, children who get angry easily and are aggressive with others tend to act impulsively. If you take a child step by step through his self-talk, you can spot the point at which he needs to inhibit his actions; then help him to foresee their outcome and explore different, more positive options.

Nine-year-old Donny came home from school with a note saying he had been fighting again on the playground and that he would be suspended next time it happened.

If Donny's mother asked him about his self-talk, Donny might say, "James grabbed the ball away from me when it was my turn. I told myself that he was mean and unfair. That made me want to hit him and I did."

Can you see the missing step? Donny goes from saying it's unfair directly into hitting. Now let's put another child into Donny's shoes. Evan is in Donny's class and the ball is grabbed from him in the same manner. Evan says, "James is mean and unfair. I had the ball. James is always grabbing from people. If I hit him, I'll just get in trouble. I think I'll tell him I want the ball back. If that doesn't work, I'll go to the teacher, and just be sure I stay away from James after this."

Both boys began to enrage themselves by labeling James "mean and unfair." But what saved Evan was that he predicted the consequences of his first impulse and thought of alternatives before he responded.

You can help children expand their self-talk to include the missing link of problem solving by leading them through the steps using either an actual or a hypothetical situation. For example, Donny's mother might ask him to remember his self-talk and then ask if he had thought ahead of time what might happen if he hit James. Did he imagine that he might get in trouble? What were some possible alternatives to hitting? She doesn't want to make Donny defensive about what he thought so she is careful to avoid an accusatory tone with him. She uses the same tone she would use with a friend she was trying to help find a solution to a problem.

Donny's mother might then suggest that next time he feels like hitting someone he could ask himself to be alert for the moment when he says to himself that the other person is mean or unfair. He should let that be his signal. Then instead of lashing out, he could ask himself, "What will happen if I hit?" Then he could ask himself how else he might solve the problem.

One way to bring home the idea of thinking about how to solve a problem before reacting is to have the child rehearse. You can make up situations and ask her to talk herself through them, using the problem-solving steps—look for options, predict consequences, and make decisions based on probable consequences.

You can also role-play with her. You might start by acting her part and talking out loud to yourself as you think of consequences and alternatives. Then switch roles: You play the offending child and have the child play herself, talking herself through the problem-solving steps aloud. You can provide the feedback and encouragement that are so important in helping a child.

POSITIVE REINFORCEMENT

If a child's efforts to control her anger go unnoticed, she is less likely to try again. One of the most effective forms of positive reinforcement is praise. Remember, however, that praise needs to be specific. Saying, "I appreciated the fact that you didn't get mad at your brother when he teased you" is much more effective than "Thanks for not fighting," because it tells the child that it was her control of her anger that you appreciated. When you know *how* she controlled it, you can be even more specific in your praise. For instance, "I noticed you take a deep breath and count to yourself just then. I think that's great. It really seemed to help you get control of your anger."

Giving rewards for self-control can also help reduce problems with anger. You can have a young child put stars on a chart or tell you whenever she feels that she has talked herself out of having a temper tantrum or striking out at someone. An older child can keep a tally of successful uses of self-talk. The child then gets rewarded for a certain number of stars or points. Younger children have more difficulty with self-control and with delayed gratification, so they need more immediate rewards than do older children. Many teachers give tokens at the end of each day that are exchangeable for prizes on a weekly basis.

Giving rewards without encouraging the child to reward or praise herself, however, misses the point. If children are to become truly self-controlled, they need to be able to evaluate their own behavior and give themselves pats on the back even when others do not. So, as you praise the child or give her points, say things like, "You must really be proud of yourself," or "I hope you give yourself a big pat on the back for that." Unfortunately, most children aren't praised for developing internal controls. Adults tend to focus more on external achievements such as grades or sports accomplishments. But internal growth is just as important.

If a child keeps track of his own efforts to conquer anger he gets a sense of making progress. He can be encouraged to be aware of how many times he felt angry and didn't blow up. Looking at those very real but seldom-noticed accomplishments is what fuels him to try harder. Many parents find that the tangible rewards they offer along with points grow less and less important to the child as he tracks his own progress.

OFFER STRESS-REDUCING TECHNIQUES

Stress often causes people to strike out in anger. Stress inoculation (pages 49–51) is a technique specifically designed to help reduce anger and fear. If you rehearse the four phases of stress inoculation with the child, he will be more able to confront and handle a stressful situation once he is in it.

Stress inoculation integrates all the kinds of positive self-talk we have discussed so far. It is involved, and it takes time and practice for a child to master it, but it is extremely effective. It should be used only with a child who has been introduced to the idea of self-talk and its effects. If you've already talked with the child about what he says to himself, and if he's open to your help, he may really enjoy rehearsing this procedure with you before a worrisome upcoming event.

This technique is appropriate only for older children who have the ability to plan ahead and think in terms of steps. Younger children need to use simpler techniques for reducing stress. For instance, a child of four or five is quite capable of taking a deep breath and counting to five before he responds in anger. (See the section on relaxation in Chapter 3 for additional suggestions.)

CONCLUSION

Learning to handle anger is a lifetime process. Few of us ever completely master our angry reactions even as adults. Moreover, sometimes anger is an appropriate and helpful emotion to have. But we don't want to be paralyzed by these feelings or act in ways that are detrimental to ourselves or others. If children learn to talk themselves through situations that make them angry, they will have a head start on life.

· 5 ·
OVERCOMING FEARS

USING SELF-TALK TO GAIN INNER SECURITY

• • •

I was afraid of almost everything as a child: the dark; monsters; ghosts; strangers; dogs; being left alone. The world was a really scary place.

When we see fear in our children, we relive our own childhood fears. If we didn't learn effective ways to deal with our own fears, it's especially challenging to help our children deal with theirs.

Fear isn't necessarily bad. It is a natural reaction to awareness or anticipation of danger. When we perceive danger, adrenaline flow prepares our body for fight or flight. Thus, fear mobilizes us to protect ourselves.

There is no way to protect a child from experiencing occasional fear. Each stage of development has its own challenges and "dangers." You cannot prevent a child from ever being in the dark, being separated from a parent, having an illness, or from other experiences that may cause fear. Nor would such an attempt be in the child's best interest. Of course, you do not intentionally expose a child to frightening experiences, but when they occur, you need to be able to deal with them openly and directly and to teach the child how to do the same.

It is not the frightening experiences themselves that are problems for a child (or an adult). It isn't even the irrational fears so characteristic of early childhood. As Selma Fraiberg explains in *The Magic Years*, her classic volume on understanding the problems of early childhood, it is the way a child manages his fears that determines their effect on his personality development. If the child's fears permeate his life so that he feels helpless and defenseless and develops an attitude of frightened submission as a result, there's a problem. If he behaves as though he were threatened by dangers on all sides so that he is constantly on guard and ready for an attack, he may develop an aggressive or defiant attitude, and that is equally problematic. He may carry these attitudes with him into adulthood and continue to be needlessly fearful or angry.

But most children overcome their irrational fears in the course of normal development. This chapter will help you understand how they do it and how self-talk plays a role in either exaggerating or lessening those fears. It will also give you concrete methods for helping yourself and your child learn to manage fear through positive self-talk.

THE RELATIONSHIP BETWEEN SELF-TALK AND FEAR

Just as every child struggles to handle anger, every child tries to overcome his irrational fears. If persistent fears dominate his life, he may have missed a crucial stage of learning: mastering the ability to talk himself through fearful situations. That ability is linked with specific kinds of self-talk.

Picture this typical childhood scene: Ten-year-old Terry has a spelling test tomorrow. Spelling is difficult for him, and he adds to his problems by saying things to himself like, "I'm no good at spelling. It doesn't matter how hard I try. I can't get it, so why try?" He puts off studying and engages in negative self-talk all the time. When he finally sits down with his mother to practice, he's primed to see every mistake he makes as proof that he can't spell. His fear and anxiety become so great that he can't concentrate, and he eventually gives up. He is anxious the entire next day. By the time the teacher gives the test, he is so panicked that he can't remember how to spell even the simplest words on the list.

Now picture the same scene: Terry has a spelling test tomorrow. He knows spelling is difficult for him, but instead of telling himself he can't do it, he says, "I'd better start studying early this evening. I know if I really concentrate and practice, I'll do okay." He practices with his mother for over an hour, and each time he makes a mistake, he reminds himself to relax and says to himself, "It's okay. Just slow down and think. Sound it out. You'll get it if you keep working at it." Not surprisingly, he does get it. By the time he and his mom finish, he feels confident that he will pass the test. Consequently, it isn't difficult for him to remind himself the next day whenever he starts to get anxious that "I studied hard. I know the words. I'll do fine." That same kind of encouraging internal dialogue continues during the test and Terry is able to concentrate and remember how to spell nearly every word.

In each case, the external situation was the same. What changed was Terry's interpretation and self-talk. In the first scene, Terry stoked his fear by telling himself he couldn't do it and interpreting his mistakes as proof of that. Through self-talk, Terry's emotions went from anxiety to panic and helplessness.

In the second scene, self-talk helped Terry manage his emotions, see his limitations objectively, and take action to overcome them.

Most of us don't act with this much maturity all of the time. Even adults can easily get caught up in interpreting events in ways that make them feel helpless, inadequate, or fearful. For young children, who have less ability to think rationally and who, in fact, *are* more helpless, coping with "dangers," real or perceived, is an even bigger challenge than it is for adults.

But it isn't only in reacting to isolated events like tests that self-talk affects fear. Gnawing anxiety, and even phobias, are related to internal speech.

When children aren't helped to work through their fears, these feelings often go underground. One young boy feared that rats lived under his house. When he mentioned his fear to his parents, they dismissed it as nonsense. There were no rats, and even if there were, rats were nothing to be afraid of, they said. Although the boy stopped talking about his fear, it didn't go away, and his internal ruminations about the rats worsened his fright. Years later, when he was an adult, his parents were shocked to discover that he had spent his early childhood in torment about the imagined rats. He outgrew the fear eventually, but he suffered needlessly for many years because no one worked with him to address his terror and to change his self-talk so that it would reassure and comfort rather than terrify him.

FEARS AND NORMAL DEVELOPMENT

Fear is a normal part of childhood. Common childhood fears include death, mutilation, and illness; animals; monsters, ghosts, witches, and other goblins; separation, abandonment, and loss of parental love; the dark; strangers; and unfamiliar situations. Charles Schaefer and Howard Millman, in *How to Help Children with Common Problems*, estimate that at least half of all children have the common fears of dogs, the dark, thunder, and ghosts, and that as many as 90 percent of children under six develop some specific fear that they ultimately outgrow naturally.

Although fears are most common between the ages of two and six, certain fears predominate at later ages. For instance, fears of physical dangers are typical from age ten up; fears related to identity issues are common during adolescence.

There are many causes of fears. First, just as with anger, children are especially prone to fear during certain stages of development, specifically during periods of disequilibrium. Second, some children are naturally more timid and fearful than others. Third, fatigue and/or illness can cause a child to be more susceptible to fear.

In addition to these internal causes, there are numerous external events that can trigger fear in a child. For example, a traumatic experience like being bitten by a dog can be the beginning of a fear of dogs or even of all animals. A parent who panics during a thunderstorm can produce a fear of storms in her child. This fear can even generalize to include fear of other natural disasters such as earthquakes, floods, hurricanes, or tornados. A home or school environment that is overly critical or demanding can lead to a child's fear of failure or disapproval.

In the course of normal development most children learn healthy ways to control and overcome their fears. Playacting, for example, can allow a young child to become the feared object (two-and-a-half-year-old Marty runs around the house "being" a vacuum cleaner) or to slay or tame an imaginary ferocious animal. Three-year-old Jeannie, for example, overcame her fear of wild animals by having an imaginary happy lion that she ordered about mercilessly.

Some children use their intelligence and ability to acquire knowledge to help them overcome their fears. Two-year-old Vincent, for instance, had no interest in toys except to take them apart. Finding out how things worked helped him feel in control. His solution to the fearful vacuum cleaner problem was not to *become* it, but rather to dismantle it. By the time he was four, he had taken apart almost every small appliance in the house. (Unfortunately for his parents he developed neither the inclination nor the ability to reassemble them until years later!)

Still other children learn early on to comfort themselves through self-talk. They put their fears into perspective by reminding themselves of their strengths, resources, and past successes; they tell themselves what they can do if the feared event takes place: "I know Mom will come and get me. She always has, but even if she forgets, I can call Daddy at work and he'll come pick me up."

Parents can do much to help children outgrow their fears by supporting whatever ways they naturally choose to overcome them. The child who engages in imaginative play, who slays dragons or tames tigers, should be allowed to do so without being lectured about how dragons don't really exist and tigers live only in the jungle or the zoo. Children who tend to go the investigative route, like Vincent, can be given things to take apart rather than simply lectured about the proper use of toys.

By preschool, most children have begun to develop self-talk. Parents can influence this development by modeling positive self-talk themselves and by guiding their children to talk positively rather than negatively to themselves.

USING POSITIVE SELF-TALK TO CONTROL FEAR

Before you can help a child change his self-talk to control his fears, you must have an idea about what his fears are and what he says to himself to maintain them.

As you observe the child, think about the common fears discussed above, listen for statements that suggest irrational fears and negative self-talk, and think about your own fears—now and in the past.

SHARING YOUR EXPERIENCE

Your children will be enthralled to hear about your childhood fears and how you conquered them by a version of self-talk. You can also tell them how you currently handle fears. This approach is especially useful when your fears are similar to theirs. Usually these fears fall into the category of psychic stress—tests/performance, mistakes, social situations—as opposed to fears of physical injury or natural events that occur more commonly in childhood.

Allison, a thirty-five-year-old mother of two, decided to take piano lessons with her eight-year-old daughter. Both Allison and her daughter enjoyed playing for themselves but were very anxious about performing in front of people. A few weeks before they were to play in a recital, Allison started talking about how she was handling her fear. She described how she used mental rehearsal (see pages 47–49) and positive self-talk: "When I start to worry about whether I will do okay, I tell myself, 'Relax. You know the piece backward and forward. If you can stay calm, you'll do just fine. And even if you make a mistake, so what? Probably no one will even know the difference.'"

Another way you can model is through the discipline you use. When adults speak to children in threatening ways, children learn to speak to themselves in ways that make them afraid. For instance, threatening to hit a child often makes the child tell himself in similar situations that he's going to get hit. This self-talk makes him fearful. Children who engage in this kind of self-talk usually do things secretly and won't admit problems to their parents or teachers because they fear retaliation or punishment.

USING AFFIRMATIONS TO OVERCOME FEAR

Affirmations help the child create the reality he wants. They are always stated positively and are most effective when his own words rather than yours are used.

You can help your child make up affirmations that program his mind to envision what he wants. If he longs to be the best basketball player on the team but gets anxious before a game, suggest that he repeat to himself that he's a good athlete and can make the plays he needs to make. It doesn't matter if he is a good player now. Repeating that to himself will be a powerful force in making it happen. When he gives himself that affirmation, he should use mental imagery to reinforce it (see Chapter 3), in a step-by-step visualization of himself playing well and making the shots he wants to make. It's important that he envision each play in detail rather than picture the team winning or himself receiving a trophy, because it is the pictures of the moves themselves that will program his mind to be able to carry them out at the time.

Here are some affirmations that can help children gain mastery over fear:

> "I'm a brave girl and I can take care of myself when I'm afraid" [or "in the dark," or "when I'm alone," and so on].
> "I can stay in bed and go to sleep all by myself."
> "I am strong and capable."
> "I don't have to let the things other people do make me afraid. I have a choice about the way I react."
> "I can face whatever I'm afraid of. It's easier to face it now than to run away from it and have to deal with it later."
> "Worrying about something never helps. I'm strong enough to stand anything that happens to me."
> "I'm the kind of person who can talk things out with other people and solve problems."

You might suggest that a child make up and use affirmations like these when he's in a difficult situation, and even start and end the day repeating positive affirmations to himself. Using the affirmations shouldn't make him feel that he was wrong for being afraid, only that he has the ability to create new feelings and to help things turn out the way he wants.

CHALLENGING NEGATIVE SELF-TALK

Challenging negative self-talk helps people to see things more objectively and rationally. Gaining perspective on a problem allows one to consider options more logically and to solve problems more satisfactorily.

It is important to remember, however, that the object of challenging negative self-talk is not to rid the child (or ourselves) of all anxiety. *Some* anxiety can be helpful. But when anxiety reaches the level of panic or an overwhelming feeling of helplessness, it disrupts one's life. Challenging negative self-talk is one way to keep it at a manageable level.

Here are some examples of negative self-statements that are often associated with some of the more common childhood (and in some cases, adult) fears. Each negative statement is followed by an example of a challenging, positive statement. These are examples only; the statements the child uses to challenge his own negative self-talk should be in his own words and should be tailored to address his particular situation.

Fear about performance (speeches, tests, athletic events, and the like)

Negative statement:

"I *have* to win" (or "get an A," or "be the best")

Challenge:

"I don't have to win. All I have to do is try my best."

Negative statement:

"I *can't*, so why try?"

Challenge:

"Just because something is hard for me doesn't mean I can't do it. If I really work at it, I can get it, but if I don't even try, I'm just chickening out. Even if I don't succeed this time, if I keep trying, eventually I'll get it."

Negative statement:

"I can't handle this; I have to quit before I fall apart."

Challenge:

"I'm stronger than I think; it's the way we react to things that makes them harder."

Negative statement:

"What if I make a mistake? People will laugh at me."

Challenge:

"Everyone makes mistakes. That's the way we learn. People might laugh at me, but probably they won't. Even if they do, I'd rather know I tried than be so afraid of people laughing that I don't even participate."

(See pages 139–143 for examples of challenges related to disapproval and rejection.)

Fear of separation

Negative statement:

"I can't make it by myself."

Challenge:

"I'm a brave kid. I can take care of myself. All these other kids are okay without their moms so I can do it, too."

Negative statement:

"What if she doesn't come back?" (or "gets in an accident," or "dies," or "forgets me")

Challenge:

"I can depend on her. She's never *not* picked me up when she said she was going to. If she's late, I'll wait a while and then go call from the office. If no one's home, I know Judy's number, and Mom always said to call her in an emergency."

Fear of the dark (and related fears of monsters, bad dreams, and so on)

Negative statement:

"If I close my eyes, something's going to get me."

Challenge:

"Keeping my eyes open doesn't do anything but keep me awake. I'm a brave girl and I can take care of myself in the dark. If I get scared, I can call Mom or Dad."

Negative statement:

"The bogeyman's in the closet and he's going to jump out at me."

Challenge:

"Mom just opened the closet and showed me it was empty, so I know there's nothing in there. I can go look again if I want to, but I think it's better if I just practice relaxing and think about all the things I can do."

Negative statement:

"I can't go to sleep. They're going to talk about me, or I'll miss something."

Challenge:

"I can go to sleep by myself. Mom and Dad have better things to do than sit around and talk about me. And even if I do miss something, so what? I'd rather miss something than feel yucky all day tomorrow because I didn't get enough sleep."

Fear of new situations

Negative statement:

"I don't know what's going to happen. Maybe I won't like it."

Challenge:

"Even when I'm in situations that I've been in before, I don't really know what's going to happen. I can handle it. In fact, it could be really fun. If I get too uncomfortable, I can always leave."

Negative statement:

"I don't do well in new situations."

Challenge:

"I certainly will never be comfortable if I don't try. Maybe I can take a friend at first and eventually, when I feel more comfortable, I'll go alone."

In general, the older the child, the easier it is for him to verbalize what his irrational ideas and negative self-talk are. Many fears of early childhood are more a function of the child's lack of control and of understanding of how the world works than they are the result of negative statements he's making to himself. Nevertheless, children as young as four or five can learn to make coping statements to themselves when they are afraid.

The challenges above are no different from coping statements except that they challenge a particular negative statement. Both share the characteristics of pointing out the child's strengths, resources, and/or past successes and putting the situation back into perspective. When appropriate, they suggest a course of action that the child could take if the dreaded situation occurred (like calling a neighbor to pick her up if her mom didn't come). They can also point out favorable things that might happen in the worst-case scenario (maybe the neighbor would take her for ice cream).

The material on pages 164–167 for helping a teenager challenge negative statements about social situations could also be used to help a child ten or older challenge negative self-talk that is fear-producing.

Younger children can at least respond to a question like, "Does that really seem like the way things are?" This approach is much more effective and less threatening than saying something like, "That's not true. You're overreacting." Remember, you want to invite the child to examine his own ideas and modify them himself.

If he sees the destructive power of his negative self-talk, he will be more likely to want to change it. Asking a question like, "Do you think saying that to yourself is making you feel more afraid?" opens the door for him to examine how his self-talk affects him.

ADDITIONAL WAYS TO USE POSITIVE SELF-TALK TO OVERCOME FEAR

Since fear and anger are both reactions to perceived danger, many of the techniques discussed in Chapter 4 are effective in handling fear as well as anger.

Use hypothetical situations

Books, movies, and TV all present opportunities to analyze the relationship between self-talk and fear and to practice replacing negative self-statements with positive ones. For example, you might say, "What do you think so-and-so is saying to herself that makes her worry? What could she say that would make her feel better?"

Making up hypothetical situations that parallel the child's experience and playing the "What If?" game is another way to give the child practice in using positive self-talk to overcome fear. For example, you might say to a nine-year-old who is anxious about tests: "Here's a story: Jake was preparing an oral report on the famous scientist Madame Curie. He was nervous about giving it in front of the class, but kept telling himself it was a whole week away. What if, all of a sudden, his teacher told him that he would have to give it two days early? What do you think he'd say to himself? How do you think the things he said would make him feel? What if Jake talked to his teacher? What would he have to say to himself to get up the courage to do that?"

"The Talking, Feeling, and Doing Game" (see page 150) is another way to present hypothetical situations.

Mutual storytelling, a technique often used by child psychotherapists, can be easily adapted by parents. The child tells a scary story. The parent then tells another version. The characters in the story act as models. They openly express their feelings, use positive self-talk to overcome their fear, and take effective action. Children learn to tell themselves similar stories and emulate the characters in similar situations.

Teach relaxation

Intense anxiety and fear interfere with clear thinking. Children can learn to think of alternatives to withdrawing (or "fleeing") when they are afraid, but not until they are calm enough to think.

The relaxation techniques described on pages 39–42 help a child get calm enough to think. Older children can learn how to inoculate themselves against fear by employing the four-step stress inoculation procedure described on pages 49–51.

Teach problem solving

Getting one's fears to a manageable level *allows* one to think, but it doesn't *teach* one to think. The natural reactions to fear are to fight, remove oneself physically or emotionally, or passively submit. You can teach the child to think about other options available to him by encouraging him to ask himself questions like:

- "What else could I do?"
- "What will happen if I do that?"
- "How will I feel about myself?"
- "How will other people feel?"

By examining his options and the probable consequences, he is free to respond in a more productive way than just fleeing from the situation.

For example, if your child wants to stay home the day of her oral report, you might ask her how staying home to avoid the report makes her feel. Does she feel brave or helpless? Then you could ask, "How else could you handle it? What other choices could you make to overcome your fear?" If you go through this process often enough with her, eventually it will become internalized and she will begin to ask herself those questions without prompting from you.

Practice

Changing old habits takes effort and practice. Structuring practice in the form of rehearsing or role-playing is especially critical when fear is involved because of the nature of fear: People (adults as well as children) are unlikely to put themselves in situations that are difficult for them or that make them anxious, but since they avoid such situations, they don't get practice in handling them. Without practice, their skills don't improve.

Having a child rehearse what she will say—both aloud and to herself—when she begins to feel afraid in a given situation helps her gain mastery and self-confidence, so that when the actual situation arises she will handle it better.

Sometimes the child may need you to act out the situation with her. This role-playing is especially helpful when fears are related to social situations. Young children, aged seven and under, often respond better to puppets than to acting out the scene themselves. They can have the puppets try several kinds of self-talk and make several different choices to see which ones work out best.

SPECIAL CONSIDERATIONS IN DEALING WITH FEAR

As we mentioned above, one of the unique characteristics of fear is that it leads to avoidance. If a child is bitten by a dog, he may avoid all dogs in the future. His self-talk convinces him that dogs are dangerous; they bite. Because he avoids them altogether, he never has the opportunity to test the accuracy of that conviction.

One way to break this cycle is to have the child engage in a pleasurable activity while in the presence of the feared object or situation. For instance, a mother might play hide and seek outside with her child in view of the neighbor's fenced dog. Or a child who was afraid of the dark might dress in a Batman costume and play out scenes with a parent in a darkened room. The child won't be saying negative things to himself when he is otherwise pleasantly engaged.

Children should never be forced to interact with a feared object or engage in a feared event. The best approach is to let the child approach the object or event gradually. To use the example of fear of dogs again: First, let the child watch someone feed the dog from behind a fence or window; then have him watch in the same room; then have him give the dog a biscuit. This gradual progression permits more and more bravery. If the child is also exposed to dogs through stories and has a chance to see and interact with dogs that are unthreatening (like puppies), the fear will decrease even more rapidly.

Another simple strategy that is often effective in helping children overcome their fears is called "paradoxical intention." It involves telling the child to pretend to become more frightened than she has ever been: "Show me just how frightened a girl might be in a thunderstorm." Then she acts out being terrified of the thunder. What often happens is that she sees her fear as being silly and begins to laugh.

CONCLUSION

Fears are a normal part of childhood, and children often come up with creative, healthy ways of dealing with them. Imaginative play, investigation, and self-talk are common solutions that frequently develop without any encouragement from adults. But when fears cause pervasive problems—as when a child develops a fearful, withdrawn attitude or an aggressive, get-them-before-they-get-me attitude—adults can teach the child to use positive self-talk to overcome fears and respond to life in a healthier, happier way.

· 6 ·
SUPERCHARGING LEARNING

• • •

Have you ever watched a toddler walk down the street, stopping to look at every object he encounters? His investigation of sidewalk life may be frustrating to the accompanying adult trying to reach a destination, but the toddler is experiencing the joy of learning.

Contrast that image with that of a third-grader in tears over his homework. All too often, the enthusiasm for learning that compels a toddler to explore every object in his path is lost by the time a child is seven or eight. As John Holt describes in his insightful observations of schoolchildren in *How Children Fail*, the most pervasive emotion that causes schoolchildren to fail is fear—fear of failure, fear of humiliation, fear of being exposed as unknowing and incompetent.

Holt writes:

> Most people don't recognize fear in children. We know when a child clings howling to his mother but subtler signs may escape us. We can take notice of telltale signs such as children's faces, voices, and gestures in their movements and ways of working that tell us that children in school are often scared, many of them scared most of the time. They learn to behave as good little soldiers, controlling their fears. However, the adjustments children make to their fears are almost all bad, and destructive of their intelligence and capacity. The scared fighter may be the best fighter, but a scared learner is always a poor learner.

In our modern humane classrooms, teachers have studied how to make learning fun and stimulating. They know they mustn't label children as slow and should not give children educational tasks that are beyond their abilities. Many teachers are now beginning to discover the role of positive self-talk in opening children's minds and defeating old ways of thinking that actually keep learning from taking place. When they teach children to use positive self-talk, they actually go to the heart of many learning problems.

In spite of advances in our educational system and thought, many children in our culture start to tell themselves at an early age that they can't learn certain things or that learning them doesn't matter. Many intelligent children act unintelligently at school because they are afraid, bored, or confused. They are afraid of failing, of being humiliated, and of being called stupid. When students were asked, "What goes through your mind when the teacher asks a question and you don't know the answer?" several students responded that they were scared to death.

The role adults play when children have learning problems too often has an effect opposite to the one intended. They pressure children to do their work, get in power struggles over homework, or offer rewards for work completed or well done. Many of these approaches are doomed to failure because they focus on the external aspects of learning, rather than the internal. They try to motivate a child from the outside. But readiness and openness to learn always come from within.

Self-talk born of fear can create a program so powerful that in spite of the child's efforts, he can't learn. Yet, without knowledge of that invisible process, the adults around him may feel helpless and frustrated. Openness to learning can occur only when children feel relaxed and at peace. Fear and its associated self-talk destroy intelligence and create poor thinking habits. If adults want to help children learn, they have to help them change their negative self-talk into positive, reassuring messages that create the peace and happiness necessary to the process. They must also put more emphasis on creating situations that allow children to learn in relaxing, open ways.

Today, a great deal of emphasis is placed on learning disabilities. But negative self-talk about learning is far more pervasive than what are typically classified as learning disabilities. Negative programming affects children who have high capacities but chronically underachieve, average children who lack enthusiasm, and children with special problems who have convinced themselves that they have to be failures. We have systematic approaches to help these children, but if a child doesn't believe that he can achieve a goal, even the most effective educational techniques aren't successful.

One professional tutor comments on the attitudes of children who are having problems with learning:

> When I get children for tutoring, they are usually very angry. They are angry at themselves for not being able to learn and for being behind. They have told themselves that they are stupid and labeled themselves in so many negative ways that it's hard to get past that. They are also angry at other people for making them do things that they no longer like to do. They may have enjoyed those activities in the beginning—like learning to read, or spell. In the beginning, those things might have even been exciting. But once they told themselves they couldn't do them, all the fun went out of them. In order to help a child open himself to learning, we have to make those activities fun again, and we have to help him start telling himself that he's a success.

This may be more difficult than it sounds. Children who have a long history of telling themselves they are going to fail don't start liking school just because adults think they should. The motivation to achieve comes from within, and lectures about how important it is to get good grades or do well in various subjects aren't effective motivators for these students.

THE ROLE OF SELF-TALK IN LEARNING AND MOTIVATION

Many adults concerned about developing a child's capacity to learn don't have a clear picture of what motivation is and how it is related to self-talk. Picture the absorption of an artist in the midst of her painting, the concentration of a scientist involved in an experiment, the involvement of an entrepreneur about to open a new business.

None of these people has to be urged to do their tasks. The compulsion to do them, and even to get lost in them so that time becomes unimportant, springs from within. These adults, like the toddler with his sidewalk exploration, have an inner drive to experiment and achieve.

How do they differ from the third-grader who is crying over her homework or the adolescent who sits listlessly in class doodling on his paper and watching the clock? What keeps them motivated in spite of setbacks, mistakes, and discouragement?

First, these people have learned that they can turn their dreams into reality or, to put it more prosaically, they know they can do what they set out to do. They have learned to tell themselves that they can achieve what they want and that the process of that achievement—not even necessarily the product—is pleasurable. The third-grader, however, has learned to discourage herself through negative self-talk that frustrates her and makes her feel incompetent. The voices of her critic and doomsayer convince her that she is incapable of mastering the material no matter how hard she tries.

Second, before they excelled in their fields, our adult examples excelled at inspirational self-talk. It's easy to imagine the kind of self-talk required to keep someone going even when the task is rigorous and he is tempted to give up. Picture, for instance, the self-talk needed by a marathon runner, a mountain climber, the head of a corporation trying to implement a new plan that everyone else says won't work.

THE VOICE OF THE INSTRUCTOR

Once one is interested in a learning task, the central voice needed is the voice of the instructor. If you want to find out how well a child is learning, you must discover how well the inner voice of his instructor works to lead him through any learning problem step by step. You can get in touch with your own voice by imagining talking yourself through a difficult recipe out loud or through street directions when you are lost.

You can hear young children instruct themselves aloud when they are building with blocks or trying to put a puzzle together. Later, as we have discussed, that self-instruction becomes internal and you hear it only when a problem is particularly difficult. Problems with all kinds of learning often occur because this voice is undeveloped and not serving its vital purpose.

When a child is having a specific learning problem, you can assess how well her inner instructor's voice is working by asking her to think out loud as she tackles the task. This will help both of you tune in to how she instructs herself. Poor learners often leap ahead. They want to finish rather than go through each step of the process. One third-grader was asked to read when she first went to tutoring. In her desire to seem accomplished, she raced through the words, distorting the syllables so that what she said was almost unintelligible. The tutor had to ask her to go back through the steps of blending sounds to make a word and then combining words to make a sentence. Listening to a child's self-instruction can clue us in to what steps are missing.

Here are a few common learning problems related to an inadequate internal instructor:

Poor retention

This is usually related to an underdeveloped inner instructor rather than negative self-talk, but you may hear evidence of the critic ("I can't remember"; "I'm no good at remembering things"; "I don't have a good memory"). The instructor's voice needs to help a child remember each step of a process. One way to help develop that retentive ability is to lead children through the steps repeatedly until they can remember them easily.

Poor concentration (child is easily distracted and has a difficult time focusing on steps of learning)

This problem is often caused by the absence of an internal instructor. If a child has not developed self-talk that helps keep him focused, poor concentration results. Children often get distracted between problems or between steps. You can help them by suggesting they tell themselves to stay on track and go on to the next step at crucial points.

Rushing through work (child is careless and doesn't give work full attention)

The voice of the instructor should lead the child through work carefully, helping him proofread for mistakes. When the instructor isn't well developed, children may rush through assignments, skipping important steps. If you help a child go through his work out loud and at a proper pace, he can develop the ability to do that internally when you aren't around. Rushing through work is also connected with the voice of the slave driver, who might say, "You've got to be the fastest." The doomsayer might also be operating to keep the child from seeing his role in what happens to him. For example, he might say, "I don't care. She'll make me do it over anyway."

Low frustration tolerance (child gets angry or frustrated when he can't figure out something right away)

In this situation you might hear, "I can't get this"; "This is stupid"; "This is too hard." Often the child believes he is stupid if he can't grasp something right away, or that learning should always be fun or easy, or that he's a failure if he makes mistakes.

The voice of the instructor talks the child through learning tasks even when he doesn't have immediate success. If that voice isn't well developed, children view the slightest setback as a sign of failure and give up easily.

DEVELOPMENTAL ISSUES

Human beings have a natural curiosity and desire to learn. The inquisitive toddler illustrates this point. But learning isn't the same for a toddler as it is for a teenager, even when the natural curiosity and enthusiasm haven't been squelched. Intellectual ability and attention span change over time. Having some understanding of the learning abilities of children at different ages can help you provide appropriate learning tasks that allow the child to be successful. Since belief in oneself is cumulative, the more successful experiences a child has, the more likely he is to develop positive attitudes and self-talk related to learning.

Young children's thinking is very concrete. What they see is what they believe. Thus, a toddler will throw a towel over his head and assume that since he can't see you, you can't see him. He'll look at the moon and assume that it is the size of a ball because that is what it looks like to him. Gradually, he learns that things aren't always as they appear.

By the time he's in early elementary school, peekaboo has turned into hide-and-go-seek and there are dim glimmerings of abstract thinking. It is a form of abstract thinking that allows him to understand that distance makes the moon appear much smaller than it is.

As his ability to think abstractly increases and he enters late elementary school, he can deal with symbols rather than concrete objects. He will be able to solve math problems without having to manipulate objects and he will gain greater and greater mastery of written language.

Concurrent with the ability to think abstractly is a tendency for the left brain to become more dominant. The natural balance that existed in early childhood between intuition and creativity on the one side and rationality and logic on the other begins to tip. By their late teens, many children have lost touch with much of their creativity and imagination. Imagery and relaxation, two techniques discussed in this chapter and elsewhere in this book, help restore that balance between the brain's functions.

Two other important aspects of cognitive development that affect learning are the change from simple to complex and the development of causal thinking. A twelve-year-old can hold several ideas and perspectives in his mind at one time, whereas a young child's thinking is egocentric—his perspective is the only one that is real to him. The preteen can consider several solutions to a problem and can make educated guesses about the probable consequences of each; the preschooler tends to be here-and-now and has difficulty connecting cause and effect.

Attention span also changes as a child gets older. Toddlers have attention spans that average less than a minute; teenagers can attend to a task (given the absence of other distractions) for almost as long as an adult. Many children get turned off from learning because their natural attention spans are not considered when the learning tasks are designed. They are required to attend to a task long after their interest has faded.

Another relevant developmental issue is the internalization of self-talk. The talk of a preschooler is as egocentric as his thoughts are. He can often be heard talking to himself. Much of that talk is self-instruction: He tells himself what to do first, what to do next, what to be careful about, and so on. As he matures, that talking to himself becomes more and more internal.

If he has heard encouragement and has heard and seen examples of positive self-talk and attitudes about learning, much of his self-talk will be helpful. For instance, if an adult who observed the child putting a difficult puzzle together comments on his efforts and how hard he worked in spite of the fact that it was difficult, then the child is likely to use those same words in his inner speech during the next difficult task. When the going gets rough, he might say, "I put together that puzzle and worked really hard even when I wanted to give up. I can do this, too."

Similarly, if adults remind a child of past achievements he may have forgotten, the child will learn to emphasize those things to himself internally.

Children are also helped to believe in their own abilities to achieve if the adults around them notice and value their interests. The fuel to achieve comes through our interest in a subject or activity. People don't all share the same interests, and some are more interested than others in academics, but if you believe in and encourage a child's interests, you can help develop his belief that he can turn dreams into reality.

One five-year-old boy decided he wanted to build himself a little shed after he saw the play *Fiddler on the Roof*. He was just learning to play the violin and he wanted to sit on the shed and practice. His parents could easily have dismissed this idea as silly. How can a five-year-old build a shed? Instead, his father gathered used lumber and worked with his son to build a tiny shed. The boy sat on the roof day after day practicing his violin. Thus began years of practicing his instrument until he achieved great competence.

Let's look now at some concrete ways you can help a child use self-talk to improve his learning potential.

USING SELF-TALK TO IMPROVE LEARNING POTENTIAL

SHARING YOUR EXPERIENCE

One characteristic shared by almost all high achievers is that they have strong models of achievement and learning. These models may be parents who worked hard and were open to learning. Sometimes they are teachers or other adults who inspire them. Often they may be characters from history. John F. Kennedy studied the political careers of Lincoln, Jefferson, and Winston Churchill. George S. Patton became absorbed in the military career of Alexander the Great at a young age and made a thorough study of his battles.

Adults influence children's attitudes about learning by the examples they provide. Do they like to read and read books for enjoyment and learning in front of their children? Do they demonstrate an interest in the world around them and show their enthusiasm for learning new things?

Look at your own self-talk about learning. What do you say to yourself about your capabilities? Do you tell yourself ahead of time that you aren't good at this kind of thing? Do you label yourself bad at puzzles or math or whatever you're trying? Sense how your internal dialogue affects your openness and feelings of competence about learning. Does it make you tense or relaxed, concentrated or discouraged or distracted?

When you finish a task, pay attention to what you say to yourself. Do you congratulate yourself for your success? Or tell yourself that you should have done it more quickly?

Do you explain how you talk yourself through a learning task? When you talk about your feelings of inadequacy and how you overcome them, you provide an important model for children who may be trying to understand how to gain mastery in a given area. You don't need to go into minute detail. But you do need to communicate the idea that in order to accomplish what they set out to do, people talk themselves through difficult tasks step by step.

One father who holds a doctorate degree told the following story: "I don't think my son had ever seen me have a hard time learning anything. He thought of me as superbright and felt I could never experience the learning problems he did. Then my wife convinced me to take a ballroom dancing class, and I had trouble learning the steps. My son used to come to the class with us and watch. He liked seeing me stumble all over myself. And he liked hearing me share how I talked myself through the steps."

TURNING ON THE VOICE OF THE INSTRUCTOR

The voice of the instructor is developed by breaking tasks down into manageable steps and taking those steps one at a time, at a pace that helps one understand the process involved.

One of the best ways to do that is to become a model of self-instruction for a child. Take a learning task that he can do without much difficulty and go through it step by step, modeling each of the self-instruction steps. First, define the task as though you were doing a jigsaw puzzle: "Let's see, what do I have to do? I have to figure out where all the pieces go. First, I'll spread them out and look at the shapes. Then I'll try one of the pieces."

Next, remind yourself to pay attention: "I'd better make sure I'm looking at all the pieces." Third, model how to handle a mistake by deliberately putting a piece in the wrong place and saying, "Oh, that piece doesn't go there. I'll have to see where else it might fit." As you place pieces appropriately, and when you finally complete the puzzle, praise yourself by saying something like, "I did it. Keep up the good work," or "Great, I put the whole puzzle together."

As a child repeats the steps out loud, give only as much help as needed. Think of yourself as a prompter backstage whose job it is to whisper key words to the actors if they forget their lines. ("What do I need to figure out now?" or "What do I need to do next?") Telling the child that you are acting like a prompter can help maintain a light, gamelike atmosphere.

BRINGING RELAXATION INTO PLAY FOR SUPERLEARNING

The ability to relax is crucial in order for learning to take place. Fear is one of the main deterrents to learning.

The antithesis of relaxation is tension. Tension is caused by fear and anxiety. Anxiety blocks learning. However, the anxiety isn't inherent in the event itself. For example, one child may approach a test situation with feelings of confidence and ease, which allow him to give his best performance. Another student who knows the material equally well may freeze simply because he sees the situation as a threat.

Dr. Thomas Tutko, author of *Sports Psyching: Playing Your Best Game All the Time*, describes the effects of anxiety when approaching a task: "Anxiety is distracting. You cannot focus your mind fully on two things at once. . . . If you are anxious, you are more likely to focus your mind on the anxiety than on the task at hand, since the anxiety—with all the body feelings it stimulates—tends to be more compelling."

Pay attention to words that indicate fear and anxiety. It is natural for children to be nervous before tests, but if that anxiety makes them worry so much that it has an impact on their performance, they need to learn to talk themselves through situations to develop calm and concentration.

You can help a child to manage situations that make him nervous by giving him words that help him relax. One of the most effective such words is simply *relax*. Explain that whenever he begins to feel anxious or tense, he can take a deep breath and exhale it slowly while saying the word *relax* to himself. (See Chapter 3 for a more complete description of this and other relaxation techniques.)

USING AFFIRMATIONS FOR LEARNING

Affirmations are especially effective in learning situations. Remember that affirmations should always be phrased in a positive way. For example, instead of saying, "I won't panic," say, "I am calm and steady."

Here are some additional examples.

Before a child studies something new, he can repeat to himself:
"I can do it."
"Now I am achieving my goals."
"Learning is something I enjoy."
"Learning and remembering are easy."

Before an exam, a child can say:
"I recognize the right answers at the right time."
"I remember all I need to know. My memory is alert; my mind is powerful."

Affirmations are powerful tools for learning because they create the kind of receptivity and calm necessary to assimilate information or demonstrate and use what has been learned. Affirmations are most effective if one can call up the emotion associated with the positive statement being made.

You can ask a child to remember a time when he had whatever feeling he is trying to achieve and to visualize it while he is saying the affirmation. Another way to call up the feeling is to have the child picture a place or call up a memory that brings about that feeling. For instance, visualizing walking through the woods, lying on the beach, or running through a meadow are common scenes that children often pick to make them feel peaceful. (These and other visualization techniques are described in Chapter 3.)

CHALLENGING NEGATIVE SELF-TALK

Children often develop habitual negative ways of talking to themselves that turn them against learning and cause fear, boredom, helplessness, or frustration. To open herself to learning or to be able to demonstrate her learning adequately, a child has to be able to refute those negative voices.

One way to help a child challenge negative self-talk that impedes his learning is to talk about hypothetical situations. You might say, "What can someone do if he tells himself he is stupid and can't learn?" The child might say, "He could tell himself that isn't true and anyone can learn if he tried." If a child is unable to refute negative self-talk, even in hypothetical situations, you should be prepared to offer suggestions. Here are some examples:

Negative statement:

"I can't do this. I'm just no good at math."

Challenge:

"Give it another try. Just because it doesn't come easily doesn't mean I'm no good at it."

Negative statement:

"What a dummy I am. I'm not going to try anymore. It doesn't do any good."

Challenge:

"Dummies are people who don't try. Making a mistake doesn't mean I'm a dummy."

Negative statement:

"This is too hard."

Challenge:

"Take it one step at a time. If I tell myself it's too hard, I'll never get it."

As with other challenges, refuting negative voices in learning situations involves trying to achieve a more balanced, realistic perspective. You might offer any of the examples above or ones you think are more appropriate for the child's particular negative self-statements, but remember that if the child can reword them so that they reflect *his* way of saying things, they will be more effective.

A teacher can help her class approach learning situations and tests more successfully by discussing common types of negative self-talk and how they impede learning. She might ask students to reveal the negative things they say to themselves and list them on the board. Then she could ask children to think of internal challenges they could make when those thoughts arise. Reinforcing these ideas repeatedly can make a dramatic difference in the comfort children feel in learning situations. It is very reassuring to know that other people have the same negative thoughts you do. More important, it is crucial to find ways of dealing with those thoughts that maximize the potential to learn.

III

HELPING THE CHILD BE SUCCESSFUL

The focus of all self-talk related to learning should be to help the child feel successful. When a child is having a problem with learning material and is getting increasingly frustrated, take him back to a level at which he feels successful. Then have him make reinforcing statements to himself ("Good, I'm working hard now") every time he completes a step. The reinforcement shouldn't be for getting it right, but for completing it. Children need to learn to appreciate their own efforts and not to feel bad if they don't always get the answer or even understand how to solve the problem right away.

Sometimes learning problems require the special attention of trained professionals. If those professionals utilize positive self-talk in their programs, they will be more effective and will also help the child feel more successful.

Focusing on self-talk takes us to the core of learning. As with the rest of life, whether one can learn a task depends less on the task itself than on the attitudes brought to it. If you can help children talk themselves through challenging learning situations, you are giving them a key to unlock their real potential.

SELF-TALK ABOUT MISTAKES

There is probably no area of learning more crucial than the way we learn to perceive our mistakes. If a child is to take chances, he has to see his mistakes as unimportant except as opportunities to learn and signals for what he should try next. If he views them as indications that he is incompetent, or feels humiliated by them, he is apt to stop trying. High achievers are not thrown by errors;

they often call mistakes by other names (glitches, bugs) just so they won't discourage themselves in the middle of a learning task.

Adults can help children by responding to mistakes in positive ways. If you take the time to talk to a child about something that he considers a failure or a mistake, you can help him to program his own self-talk to be more positive. For example, a child who is frustrated because her first try at a math problem failed might be told, "Oh, that way of doing it didn't work. So now you know that you need to try something else."

Contrast this with a less healthy, but perhaps more common, way of responding to mistakes: "What's the matter with you? Are you paying attention to what you're doing? That answer is wrong. Now sit up and try harder this time." This second type of response would make most children and adults want to leave the problem behind. Moreover, if a child starts repeating these kinds of statements to himself, he will quickly become discouraged when a mistake occurs. He will decide that the problem is his own inadequacy and lose any determination to persevere. Eventually, he will not even try if he thinks there's a chance he may fail or make mistakes.

When a child makes a mistake, or you make a mistake in front of him, it might help to imagine that you are responding to more than the moment. Try to picture yourself programming the child to have attitudes toward future mistakes through the things you say about a particular error.

CONCLUSION

Self-talk is an integral part of learning. Successful learners know how to talk themselves through complex tasks, monitor their progress, and provide themselves with encouragement. They engage in inspirational self-talk and remind themselves that they can achieve whatever they set out to achieve if they just keep trying. They don't expect learning to be easy, nor do they interpret mistakes as evidence that they are stupid, inadequate, or incapable.

Any child can learn to use self-talk to help him reach his full learning potential. Adults can be instrumental in this process when they model positive self-talk and attitudes about learning, teach the child to make positive affirmations and to challenge his negative self-talk, and help him learn to instruct himself and relax so that his anxiety doesn't interfere with his concentration.

·7·
SELF-TALK AND SPORTS AND GAMES

• • •

Malcolm opens the door and throws his books on the kitchen floor. When his mother asks him to pick them up, he stomps off. Later he reveals the cause of his distress. He was one of the last people picked for the baseball team in his fourth-grade class. He felt humiliated, and when he got up to bat he struck out just because he was so upset. "I'm usually a good player, but I'm sure I won't be able to hit the ball now that I know no one wants me on their team."

Sarah gets a stomachache every time she goes to a swim meet. Her mother tries to persuade her to eat before the meet but she protests that she will get sick because she is too nervous. Not eating only makes her digestive problems worse, and her stomach pains then make her fear that she won't be able to swim in the meet.

Bobby has been under stress since the beginning of football season. The coach has pressured the team so much about winning that Bobby doesn't enjoy going to practice anymore. He complains that football is no longer fun.

Positive self-talk is now recognized as a vital resource for improving athletic performance, controlling pre-performance anxiety, and increasing the enjoyment of sports activities. The field of sports psychology has made the public aware that athletic performance is conditioned as much by mental attitudes as by physical skill. This is true on every level of athletic endeavor. Positive self-talk is as important for professional athletes as for the children in the examples above.

A professional ballplayer is just as likely as Malcolm to strike out if his self-esteem has received a blow. Many athletes—amateur and professional—are like Sarah and suffer from stress-related illnesses that they can't control. Involvement in sports at any age is likely to cause some tension and apprehension unless the players have learned techniques for using their minds to leave worry behind and create a better performance.

Today the high-tension atmosphere of children's sports causes more anxieties and stress-related illnesses than occurred in the past. Where children once played ball on a corner lot for enjoyment, the world of Little League, sports camps, and adult participation has changed the experience of childhood games and sports. Children are urged to be goal-directed, skill-oriented, and competitive rather than to just have fun. Although children themselves may enjoy the stimulation of adult-organized sports, the attitudes that permeate those situations often cause certain challenges.

Children must deal with pressures to win from adults as well as teammates and peers, in addition to problems with their own self-esteem when things don't go right. Positive self-talk and other techniques that focus on the power of the mind to build physical skill have proved effective with the whole range of sports participants, from elementary-school soccer and swimming teams to Olympic medalists.

CHALLENGES OF SPORTS

The challenge of sports at any level is to give maximum performance under the most extreme pressure. No matter what the tensions and events in the playing arena, the player has to be able to manage his own self-talk so that he can keep his concentration on what he has to do next. The anxiety created by negative self-talk can detract from performance and cause confusion. For most children, participation in sports activities can be highly charged and emotional, with all kinds of issues like winning and losing, the esteem of other players, anger about decisions made, the fairness of other players, and so on.

It is a major challenge for children to be able to manage the emotions and anxiety of sports events in socially acceptable ways. Using the body to keep the mind relaxed is to perform successfully in sports; when a player is tense, his game suffers. Since most sports are full of the strain of trying to win, it is only through mental control that relaxation can occur in the midst of playing.

In *Sports Psyching*, Dr. Thomas Tutko advises his readers about this condition:

This state of relaxed concentration is not some sort of exotic trance—nothing you've never done before—but a way of keeping anxiety from getting the upper hand so you can better channel the energy of the game's excitement into productive performance. You may still become anxious during competition, of course, but at least now the emotions that are always a part of sports will add to the excitement of your game rather than destroy it.

You cannot focus your mind fully on two things at once. When you need to pay attention to a certain play you can't be worrying about the last one or the one coming next. But if you are anxious, you are more likely to focus your mind on the anxiety than on the task at hand, since the anxiety—with all the body feelings it stimulates—tends to be more compelling.

DEVELOPMENT AND SPORTS

Young children need to develop basic large- and small-muscle skills for sports activities. Pushing children into sports before they have the physical readiness, concentration, or cognitive ability to remember rules is apt to make them anxious and less confident in their participation later on.

Young children are not always articulate about their feelings and may not be able to express the tensions they feel in sports situations. Since their social skills aren't well developed, competitive activities often end in tears or aggression. But elementary-school children are capable of using self-talk and other techniques to improve their ability to work with others as well as their performance.

TECHNIQUES FOR APPLYING SELF-TALK TO SPORTS

MODELING

Adults affect children's ability to maintain relaxation and equilibrium through the things they say about the game. If they pressure ("Keep your eye on the ball"; "Don't fumble it now") then the child or young person is apt to admonish himself, which will distract him, make him nervous, and keep him from playing better.

It is helpful for adults to remember that the primary purpose of any game is enjoyment, not being best, or winning, or even developing skill. If they can keep that perspective, they can help children deal with the internal and external pressures.

Adults can also model positive self-talk by sharing the ways they currently approach situations in sports. If they don't participate in sports they can talk about other competitive or demanding situations.

A father who plays racquetball might say, "When I'm on the court I tell myself it doesn't matter who wins. I'm just out there for enjoyment and exercise. When I get all caught up in winning, sometimes I don't even play my best game. It's more important for me to enjoy playing and feel I'm doing my best than to score points."

You can also program a child's self-talk by commenting on things that aren't involved with winning or competition. You might say, "You know, you looked as though you were really enjoying yourself out there; that's what counts," or "When you made that play you looked as if you had more confidence than you've had in other games." The object is to bolster the child's self-esteem, not to offer criticisms to improve his performance.

Adults need to help children develop the voices of the encourager and nurturer in sports.

Children may push themselves beyond their limits. You can encourage children to pay attention to bodily signals that they need to rest or be alert for any pain that might signal injury. If you say, "I think you've worked hard and deserve a break," it will help your child to say that to herself. It will also help her to assert herself with teammates and pressuring coaches if she feels they are pushing her beyond her endurance.

SPORTS PSYCHOLOGY

The central techniques outlined in sports psychology focus on four areas: breathing (relaxation), concentration, and mental rehearsal and physical practice. Children interested in improving their abilities in any sport can use positive self-talk to work on all of these areas.

Breathing

"One way to break up any kind of tension is good deep breathing," says golfer Byron Nelson. Nervousness tends to constrict the muscles in the diaphragm, chest, and throat, and this tightening makes breathing more shallow and rapid. If a child is exerting himself, he needs more air, yet he is getting less because of nervousness. Having too little breath makes one feel out of control and can lead to panic.

Release from tension means freedom to breathe. Children need to learn about the role breathing plays in their ability to perform, and remind themselves that they can breathe freely and deeply, and remind themselves that they have to remember to breathe.

Concentration

Participation in sports is a wonderful way for children to learn about concentration, but it does not develop automatically. Children have to learn about concentration. To be concentrated is to be single-minded—to focus all one's attention on one thing. In our culture, where households commonly have TVs and radios blaring when children are studying, concentration is not usually learned systematically. One has to practice focusing on something for sustained periods of time without letting the mind wander. Concentration keeps out distractions.

Children often experience natural concentration when they are absorbed in an activity that they like. They might work on a puzzle or a drawing for hours, not even noticing how much time has elapsed. Adults can help children develop that natural focus through sports activities. They can learn to shut out distractions at will if they are willing to experiment with concentrating and on its effects.

Tutko shares a story about a college basketball center who was an excellent player but had problems when he stood at the free-throw line. It was hard for him to sink a foul shot because he felt self-conscious about his extraordinary height when he stood in that position. To overcome the problem, he would sit by himself before every game and imagine the rim of the basket, concentrating totally on his image of it. Then, when he stood at the free-throw line, just looking at the rim would bring back that concentration and shut out his feeling of self-consciousness.

One of the things professional players do is practice concentration exercises outside of the game to improve their abilities. Children can do the same exercises and if they stick with them their concentration should improve remarkably. They need to start by focusing on a real object, or even a picture of one. Preferably the item would be related to the sport or game, such as a tennis ball or golf ball, a picture of a sports field or a swimming pool, but the process of concentrating matters more than the object itself.

If a child is motivated to improve her concentration in the game, she should set aside a certain period of time every day —perhaps five or ten minutes, depending on her age. She should go through a short period of relaxation first and then concentrate on her object. While she is concentrating she can say the name of the object, for instance, *ball*. Repeating this word keeps her mind from wandering.

She should begin to examine the ball or other object visually in every detail. If she's focusing on a real object, not a picture of one, she should feel its weight, texture, and so on, looking at it from different angles. If it is a photograph she should just concentrate on the details. If her concentration breaks she can say to herself, "I have been concentrating on the ball. This is what it feels like to be concentrating. I am relaxed. I feel good. My attention is totally focused on the ball."

She can then say her word of concentration again: *ball*. You should explain to the child that professional athletes use these exercises, but they take practice. At first her mind will fill with distracting thoughts, but she shouldn't give up. After a while, she will learn to turn her thoughts back to the ball when her mind wanders. This is the beginning of real concentration.

Mental rehearsal

Mental rehearsal is different from concentration, but concentration is required in order to do it successfully. Mental rehearsal is not daydreaming about a future game. It is picturing in advance precisely what moves and responses one ideally wants to make.

In mental rehearsal a player thinks about the game and the specific plays that may occur. In his mind, he responds to the various moves and countermoves as he would in real life, imagining successful completion of the play. The more vivid his imagination is, the better. He should call up every aspect of the play.

Jack Nicklaus, the famous golfer, calls mental rehearsal "going to the movies." He imagines each shot from start to finish before he actually makes it, mentally setting up, swinging, hitting the ball, seeing it take off, land, and roll to a stop.

Children can learn to use mental rehearsal more effectively by chronicling what they do through self-talk. They can learn to keep their minds on the rehearsal by saying, "Now I'm picking up the bat. Then I hold it in position. Now I look at the pitcher. Now I focus on the ball. Now I swing." Going through each step verbally ensures that they don't skip any steps. The goal of mental rehearsal is to make those moves automatic when they occur during the tension of the game. Using mental rehearsal in sports can help children use it in other areas of life.

Physical practice

The goal of physical practice, like mental rehearsal, is to make moves automatic. Mental practice can help that process along. A child can repeat the same phrases and thus call up the images he has used.

PLAYING HIS OWN GAME

All of the above techniques are aimed at helping a child to enhance his physical skills by using his mind to support that process. However, games are not played on just a physical level. Sports also require children to respond to each other psychologically and socially in emotionally charged situations. One child may make fun of another. He may use one-upmanship by bragging about his own skill or better equipment. He may actually ridicule others and call them names.

Self-talk can help a child maintain his internal equilibrium in spite of what anyone else on the playing field does or says. The goal in sports is always to focus concentration on the play of the moment—not on the play that just occurred, the comment made by an opposing player, or one's own anxiety about what will happen next.

Tutko calls this focus, and the ignoring of distractions, "playing your own game." The premise is that to maintain concentration players must learn to shut out what other people say as well as the negative things they say to themselves. You can explain to a child that he can hang onto his equilibrium by telling himself he is playing his own game. He doesn't need to get distracted by other people. He can only play to the best of his ability, and his job is to remind himself that even when he gets thrown off balance he can and will do that.

A child who is challenged by other players can say things

to himself like, "I'm going to ignore that. He's just trying to psych me out. I'm playing my own game and need to concentrate."

USING AFFIRMATIONS FOR PEAK ATHLETIC PERFORMANCE

Affirmations are important in sports and can even support a child's ability to rehearse mentally or physically.

A child might couple a mental rehearsal with a statement like, "I will respond the way I want when I am playing."

She might use an affirmation during physical practice like, "My arm is strong and I can make the moves I want."

Affirmations can also be used before a game. A child or young person might repeat phrases like these:

"My mind is calm and steady. I will be playing my best today."

"I am a good soccer player. My mind is clear and I am full of energy."

"I can use my concentration to play better and make the plays I want."

AVOIDING NEGATIVE SELF-TALK IN SPORTS

One of the worst opponents of a player in any sports event is negative self-talk. The things a child or young person says to himself about his performance can unbalance him more than any remark by another player. Here are some situations that may call up negative voices, and the challenges a child might make in response.

Bungling a play:

"What are my teammates going to think? I don't deserve to be on the team."

Challenge:

"It doesn't matter what mistakes I make. Everyone makes mistakes. All that matters is having fun and concentrating on the next play."

Being taunted by another player:

"I'd better watch out. He's probably much better than I am. I'm sure to lose now."

Challenge:

"I'm a good player. He's just trying to throw me off my game and I won't let him."

Feeling nervous before a play:

"What if I can't hit the ball? I'm sure I'll blow it."

Challenge:

"It's natural to be nervous. I can use that energy to play better."

Sports is an ideal area of life in which to practice and study the effects of self-talk. Since so many athletes have used self-talk to their advantage, children are often motivated to follow their example. However, children's efforts need to be reinforced. They should be praised for practicing concentration or mental rehearsal techniques, and for using self-talk to maintain calmness and balance. They need to understand that positive results can occur only through patience and repetition, and they shouldn't give up if they don't achieve instant results. The same self-supportive techniques they master for sports participation can help them perform better in other areas, too.

· 8 ·

MAKING FRIENDS

USING SELF-TALK TO FORM AND
MAINTAIN SATISFYING RELATIONSHIPS
IN EARLY AND MIDDLE CHILDHOOD

■ ■ ■

An incident from my childhood still stands out in my mind. I had moved away and I went back after several months to visit my two best friends. They made it clear that they had formed a bond that didn't include me anymore. They would whisper to each other and they walked with their arms around each other, leaving me to walk alone. I felt so bad. But I told myself that I had new friends and didn't have to focus on the past.

—*Ariel, mother of three children*

Learning how to make friends and relate to others is one of the biggest challenges of childhood. During the ups and downs of this learning, children can experience rejection and failure. You can probably recall at least one painful memory involving a friend or classmate. Can you remember feeling rejected? Being teased? Being falsely accused? Feeling betrayed?

Children do things to one another that often seem primitive, like whispering in front of other people and hitting and shoving when they are angry. And they say things like, "I don't like you anymore," "You can't come to my birthday party," or "You're stupid."

When you stop and think about how complex social interaction is—all the nuances of language, all the nonverbal cues, the thoughts, feelings, and intentions people try to convey—it isn't surprising that children's relationship skills seem pretty undeveloped. They are social novices with a lot to learn.

Although everyone survives the blows of childhood relationships and goes on to kinder, more considerate ways of treating others, some emerge with a sense of self-worth and others with a sense of being socially inept and unlovable. How one emerges depends to a great extent on whether one has learned to *talk oneself through relationships in helpful ways*. When Ariel had her painful childhood encounter with old friends, she was able to put the hurt in perspective by telling herself that she could focus on the new, positive relationships in her life.

THE ROLE OF SELF-TALK IN RELATIONSHIPS

David's fifth-grade classmates think of him as a bully. If he can't be the first to bat, he pushes his teammates down. If he can't butt into the cafeteria line, he shoves those in front. David's self-talk contributes to his problem. First, David has grown up bullying his younger brother. He says the same things inside his head that he says to his brother out loud: "You do it because I said so. I'm bigger than you, and if you don't, you'll be sorry." Second, when people don't do what David wants, he tells himself that the world is unfair, which makes him angry. The voice of his inflamer tells him to teach these guys a lesson and he lashes out.

Five-year-old Danny has a similar problem. He hits and pushes his preschool classmates who have what he wants, whether it's a toy or a place at the table. But Danny's *internal* process is different from David's. Danny doesn't feel angry or vengeful; he doesn't think at all. Like many young children with impulse problems, Danny hasn't learned to think before he acts. His thoughts don't mediate his actions as do the thoughts of most older children. When his desires are thwarted, he just strikes out without any thought about the consequences or whether there might be a better way to handle the situation.

Cindy has another kind of social problem. She is so shy that she doesn't really make friends. Cindy feels more comfortable with adults than children. At lunchtime, she sits with the teacher instead of joining the other children. Most of Cindy's self-talk comes from her critic. She tends to say things to herself like, "No one wants to play with me, I'm no good at games. Why ask?" If she does approach someone, she is self-conscious about everything she does, and says things to herself like, "Why did I say something so dumb?" She also tells herself that if someone rejects her, it means she's a nerd. Saying these things to herself (consciously or unconsciously) makes Cindy withdraw from others. If she could endure an occasional, inevitable rejection and not let it affect her sense of self-worth, she could join in with other children.

These three children could have more satisfying relationships if they learned new forms of self-talk.

David could be helped if he were taught to remind himself that it's OK if other people don't always want to do what he wants, and that he doesn't have to get angry about it. He could learn to make more realistic statements to himself, like, "He might want to do it my way and he might not. Maybe we could take turns." David also needs to develop empathy. He could make friends more easily if he could talk himself through what others might be thinking. If he could learn to stop and ask himself, "How would I feel if someone did that to me?" he could stop his bullying. He might make self-statements like, "People don't like to be told what to do," or "People don't like their place in line taken." This type of self-talk would play an important role in helping him to control his anger and act more considerately toward others.

Danny needs to start from ground zero in terms of thinking through social situations. He can learn to tell himself to stop and think before he lashes out at someone. Then he could ask himself, "How would I feel if someone did that to me?" Like David, he might learn to make self-statements like, "People don't like to be told what to do" or "People don't like their place in line taken." Self-talk like this would help him to control his impulses and be more considerate. But Danny also needs to ask himself, "How else can I handle this?" Answering this question would give him practice in generating nonviolent solutions to problems. His teacher can help by talking about hypothetical situations with the class so that all the children start thinking about gentler ways to get what they want. Such practice will help Danny think about the consequences of various options he might choose, something he presently completely neglects to do. It will also help him learn that not everyone can get what they want all the time and that compromise and negotiation are often necessary.

Cindy could use self-talk to give her courage. Instead of thinking that each encounter with someone is crucial for her well-being, she could say things to herself like, "Maybe it will work out to ask if I can play and maybe it won't, but I'm going to try." Telling herself that not everyone has a best friend or that others feel lonely, too, might help her feel less isolated. She might try saying things to herself like, "I bet she's looking for someone to play with, too." This positive self-talk could inspire her confidence.

Your child may not have social problems as pronounced as these, but she can probably still use some help in learning to talk to herself in positive ways. Changing her self-talk can make her relationships more satisfying and help her overcome social problems.

Self-talk plays a vital role in relationships throughout life. People who learn in childhood to talk to themselves in positive, rational ways are ahead of the game. Self-talk can determine how we interpret other people's communication and body language, the way we approach or avoid others, how we handle conflicts and intimacy, our reactions to what other people do, how we think others view us, the images and expectations we have of others, and more.

Let's look at some common irrational ideas adults have about friendships.

WHY YOU REACT THE WAY YOU DO

Childhood friendships can confuse us. Have you ever been annoyed at your child's best friend for treating her badly, or resented other kids for leaving your child out? Adults often react strongly to conflicts among children.

But if you look at children's relationships objectively, you can help and guide them more effectively. It's not possible to do that unless you understand how your own thinking about childhood friendships colors your current perceptions.

Many adults' ideas about friendship developed in childhood. One such notion is that childhood friendships should be different—no one should get rejected, or feel unpopular. Of course parents would like to make this an ideal world, in which friendships are conflict-free and cliques are abolished. As this is not possible, the objective adult will try to help children deal with the world the way it is. Discomfort is inherent in growth. To embrace the idea that all pain should be eliminated is unrealistic and perhaps counterproductive. As the saying goes, "The pearl caused the oyster great pain."

Another common irrational idea about friendship is that there is a *right* way to do it: "You should have a best friend"; "You should have lots of friends"; or "You should be outgoing and able to make friends easily."

In truth, however, not everyone has a best friend, nor does everyone need one. By the same token, not everyone has lots of friends. In reality, people have different friendship patterns determined by their personalities, social skills, and needs.

Adults unconsciously communicate these and similar irrational ideas to children with the intention of protecting them. Unfortunately, when it comes to relationships—child or adult—there is no such thing as avoiding hurt and risks. The ups and downs of friendship are part of learning to be more sensitive to others, learning to communicate effectively and considerately, and learning to express feelings in ways that others can understand and appreciate.

THE DEVELOPMENT OF SOCIAL SKILLS

Young children preschool age and below lack specific cognitive skills that are crucial for smooth social interaction. For instance, they are egocentric in their thinking, meaning they assume others see things as they do. Most can't even consider another perspective, let alone hold two perspectives in their minds simultaneously. Even more alien to them is the skill of finding compromises or solutions that will satisfy both parties in a conflict situation.

A typical two-and-a-half- or three-year-old's solution to someone's grabbing his toy is simply to grab it back. He can't understand that the other child wants it, too, so how can he come up with a solution like taking turns? If you ask him what should be done, he'll probably say, "He should give it back," because his own needs are all he is aware of.

Similarly, preschoolers have little ability to empathize, or to grasp cause and effect. They need to be asked repeatedly questions like, "How would you feel if you were using a toy and someone grabbed it?" before they see that their actions have effects—both emotional and otherwise—on others.

Helping young children develop the ability to form and maintain healthy relationships does not necessarily involve teaching them to use positive self-talk per se. Instead, adults need to help them interact with others successfully. Specifically, this means helping them identify and label their own feelings, understand how other people might feel in a given situation, and understand the effects of their behavior on others.

Adults often need to provide preschoolers with rules and solutions to conflicts. Of course, the ultimate object is for the child to be able to solve his own problems, but he needs guidance and information before he is able to do that independently. Thus, you might need to suggest to two three-year-olds fighting over a toy that they take turns, but by the time they're five, you should be able to ask, "How can we solve this problem?" rather than give them a ready-made solution.

How adults respond to children's social situations forms

the basis of the children's views of friendships and what they say to themselves about relationships. Compare these two scenes:

Three-year-old Jessica is intentionally knocked down by one of her playmates for no apparent reason. The day-care provider swoops down to comfort her and says that Jessica's friend is bad and Jessica doesn't need to play with her anymore. The message to Jessica: Certain people are bad and you should stay away from them. If the adults in Jessica's life continue this pattern, Jessica is likely to begin to see the world as a dangerous place and herself as having no defense but to withdraw.

In the second scene, the day-care provider talks to the offending child and explains, "That hurt Jessica. We don't knock people down. Be gentle." And she shows the child how to hug a friend. The adult comforts Jessica, but since Jessica isn't physically hurt, she doesn't remove her or tell her to stop playing with the other child. Instead, she watches from a distance and intervenes only as much as is necessary to protect Jessica from actual harm. The message Jessica gets: It is wrong to knock people down; treat people gently; I can take care of myself, but adults will be there if I need them. With this continued kind of support, Jessica will probably come to believe she is able to take care of herself socially and will know what is appropriate social behavior and what is not.

As children's cognitive abilities and social experiences increase, adults can intervene more directly to help them develop positive self-talk. Children as young as five or six can control impulsive behavior by thinking through a problem (that is, by identifying the problem, generating solutions, examining possible consequences, and developing a plan of action). They can be taught to use positive affirmations and to challenge negative self-talk.

USING POSITIVE SELF-TALK IN SOCIAL SITUATIONS

Three types of social situations are commonly helped by positive self-talk: 1) initiating relationships and trying to make friends; 2) coping with rejection, disapproval, or social failure; and 3) using negotiation or self-control to cope with conflict. Let's look at examples of how to use positive self-talk in each situation.

SELF-TALK TO HELP CHILDREN INITIATE NEW RELATIONSHIPS

Modeling

If you notice that a child hangs back when she doesn't know other children well, you might introduce yourself and start a conversation with someone in her presence. She will see how you do it, and if you share your self-talk with her, she will also see how she might talk to herself in similar situations.

Sam had taught fourth grade at the same school for ten years. He seldom talked to his colleagues, and he kept pretty much to himself, but he was a very caring, competent teacher. When he noticed that Cindy (whom we introduced earlier) never interacted with her peers on the playground, he started making an effort to initiate contact with other people when she was around. Cindy always hung on him when he had recess duty, so he had plenty of opportunities to show her how he talked himself through making contact with others. When he saw the student teacher come out of the classroom, for instance, he said, "I usually don't try to make friends with people, but I know she's new and feeling a little left out, so I'm going to go talk to her. I just have to keep reminding myself that she won't bite and that she'll appreciate having someone to talk to."

You could also tell a child who hesitates to make social contact that you find it difficult to make new friends, too, but that you tell yourself that most people are really nice and that they're probably shy, too.

Similarly, you can share the feelings you had as a child about meeting new people and explain how you talked to yourself to overcome your shyness.

Affirmations

Affirmations are an effective way for children to reprogram themselves to have more successful relationships. They can sometimes prevent negative self-talk by repeating affirmations to themselves before they get into difficult situations. This increases their self-confidence and produces a positive attitude that encourages them to initiate friendships. Here are some examples of affirmations that would be appropriate for children seven or eight and older:

"I am an attractive, likable person."
"I can meet new people."

"I like getting to know people, and people like getting to know me."

"I remember how to make conversation and let someone know I am interested in them."

Younger children might say simpler things to themselves, such as:

"I think I can." (*The Little Engine That Could* is the reference.)
"I can do it."

When Cindy's mom and Sam had a conference, they discussed their mutual concern about Cindy's shyness. Cindy's mother talked about affirmations with Cindy and described how they had helped her get over her fear of talking to customers on the phone at work. Cindy decided she would try using affirmations to help her approach people.

At first, Cindy chose "I'm the most popular girl in the class" and "People love to talk to me." After a couple of weeks, however, she realized that she really didn't care about being the most popular girl in the class but that she *did* want to be comfortable talking to new people. Then she started saying to herself, "I am comfortable talking to new people," "People really like me," and "People love to talk to me."

Cindy repeated her affirmations daily—upon first awakening, at bedtime, and several times during the day. She found that if she used them when she was feeling fairly relaxed and peaceful, they gave her courage and self-confidence. Once she was in a difficult situation and was already feeling scared, they weren't very helpful. For those situations, Cindy learned to challenge her negative self-talk.

Challenging negative self-talk

If you have already pinpointed that a child has problems initiating friendships, you may also be aware of some of the negative things she tells herself. Typically, people have trouble initiating contact with others because they either 1) fear rejection, or 2) fear making fools of themselves. Those fears are often fed by such negative self-statements as:

"What if she's mean to me?"
"What if I go up and introduce myself and he just ignores me?"
"I wouldn't know what to say; I'd just make a fool of myself."

Children as young as five or six can be taught to challenge these statements once they become aware of them. Challenges for the above statements might be:

"Most people are nice. Even if she isn't interested in becoming my friend, at least I've tried to be nice. There are plenty of other people I can make friends with."
"The chances aren't very good that he'll ignore me, and even if he did, it wouldn't be the end of the world. It would just mean he wasn't someone I really wanted to make friends with."
"I can practice what to say. Asking questions always shows you're interested. Whatever I do, if he's someone I would want as a friend, he will understand; if he isn't and thinks I'm a fool, I don't really care."

A common characteristic of effective challenges related to initiating friendships is that they reduce the need for every attempt to meet with success. They concede that, in fact, the person might *not* respond favorably or one *might* get tongue-tied; but they challenge the underlying belief that it would be disastrous if that happened. Since some attempts to make friends are bound to be unsuccessful, children need to learn to roll with the punches and not interpret the "failures" as evidence that they are unlovable or unfit for social contact.

SELF-TALK TO HELP CHILDREN DEAL WITH REJECTION AND DISAPPROVAL

While only a few children are plagued with the problem of shyness or reticence in meeting new people, most experience difficulties with situations that involve rejection or disapproval by someone they consider a friend. Self-talk can be an invaluable tool for helping a child understand and work with those situations.

Modeling

Some children are especially sensitive to disapproval and rejection. They interpret everyday occurrences—someone disagreeing with them, refusing to do what they want, or ignoring them—as rebuffs.

Since these setbacks happen frequently to everyone, you will have lots of opportunities to model how positive self-talk can help. First it's useful to find out how the child reacts to rejection. With anger? Hurt? Self-deprecation? If you can't be sure, think about the things you say to *yourself* in such circumstances. If you react with anger, you probably say something like, "I'll teach him for making me feel bad." If you feel hurt, you might say, "How could she do this to me?" If self-deprecation is more your style, you may say, "I must be lacking; it's probably my fault she doesn't approve of me."

As you begin to change what you say to yourself, tell the child what you are learning so she can benefit from your example.

Young children won't be able to grasp subtle nuances of adult interactions, but they can relate to situations that parallel their own experiences. For example:

- If you ask a friend to come over and she has "other plans," you can say, out loud so the child can hear, "I used to get all upset about stuff like that, but now I just tell myself I have lots of other friends I can ask, and that just because she can't come, it doesn't mean she doesn't like me."
- If your spouse snaps at you for no apparent reason when he comes in the door from work, you might say, "Sometimes I forget that Dad needs to be left alone for a few minutes after he gets home from work. I have to remind myself that it won't do any good to snap back or get angry or tell myself he isn't being fair. It just means he needs some time alone for a while."

Danny (whom we introduced earlier) watched his dad and finally learned to stop and think rather than lash out when he was frustrated. As soon as Danny's dad became aware of his son's problem, he started modeling self-control. Rather than yell at people when he was angry, he started counting to three and telling himself: "Calm down," and "Think before you react." Sometimes, especially when other family members were involved, he would say these things out loud so Danny could hear. At other times, for instance when speaking to business associates on the phone, he would talk to himself silently and afterward say something to Danny like, "I almost lost my cool, Dan, but I knew that would only make things worse. So I just took a deep breath and told myself to calm down. That really helps. I get along much better with people when I remember to do that."

Affirmations

Affirmations that help children deal with rejection and disapproval focus on strength and one's ability to handle life:

"I am a strong, likable person."
"I can deal with whatever comes my way."
"I can handle things."
"I am brave."

These are appropriate for children four years old and up. As with other kinds of affirmations, they should be stated positively and in the child's words. They should reflect the child's goals for himself, not necessarily how you want him to be.

Don't worry if the affirmations aren't specific. In this case, a vague "I can handle whatever comes my way" would probably be more effective than "I can handle it when people aren't nice to me." The latter, more specific statement keeps the child focused on the fact that "people aren't nice" to him. Taking people's reactions too personally is part of the problem, and this statement just reinforces that perception.

Challenging negative self-talk

Again, you need to understand how the child responds in order to help him challenge his negative self-talk. Does he see rejection as a personal failure or as evidence that the world is unfair or that he might as well give up or that he'd better fight back?

For example, if your child interprets criticism as a personal attack, he will probably come home in tears if his teacher says his work is sloppy. You can translate the teacher's comments into realistic terms that make it seem less personal. You might say, "I think she means you have to stay on the lines and try to make all your letters the same size. Also, things look tidier when you try to erase neatly. When you're doing your work, you might try to remind yourself every few minutes to check your paper for neatness. It doesn't mean *you're* sloppy."

A child who gets angry when she feels rejected can be taught to use self-talk to gain self-control. Annie consistently got angry with her friends, so they became wary of asking her over. When her feelings got hurt or she felt left out, she would leave. Sometimes she even stomped out of the house and walked home. Annie's mother helped her by asking her what she said to herself in those situations. Annie responded that she told herself her friends were unfair—that they never wanted to do what she wanted and always wanted their own way. Her mother asked Annie, "If people don't do what you want, do you think they are unfair or don't like you?" Annie didn't know. But her mother suggested that she might try something different in situations that weren't working for her, like saying, "People don't have to do what I want and, if they don't, it doesn't mean they don't like me."

Annie's response contained some red flags, *never* and *always*, that suggested she was overgeneralizing. Other words that give this kind of distorted thinking away are *no one* and *everybody*. If overgeneralizing is the basis for a child's sensitivity to rejection and disapproval, you will hear repeated laments such as:

"No one likes me."
"Nobody wants to play with me."
"Everybody hates me."
"Everyone makes fun of me."

Children can learn to see things in a more flexible way, by changing their self-talk. Challenges for this kind of negative self-talk address the overgeneralization directly. For example, challenges for the above statements might be:

"It's not true that *nobody* likes me. Some people like me; some don't. If I'm nice to people, most people will like me."
"Just because one person doesn't want to play with me doesn't mean *no* one wants to play with me. I'll just keep asking until someone says yes."
"Joey said he hated me because he was mad. I say that when I'm mad, too. He doesn't really hate me, and it certainly isn't true that *everybody* hates me."
"I don't like being teased, but it's not the end of the world. I have lots of friends who never tease me, so I'll just try to hang around them more and stay away from the kids who tease me a lot."

SELF-TALK TO HELP CHILDREN NEGOTIATE AND WORK OUT CONFLICTS

Conflicts are an inevitable part of friendships. A child who learns how to negotiate and compromise will have happier, more successful relationships throughout life. There is much you can do to help a child learn how to deal with conflicts.

Modeling

Many adults have the misconception that they should never disagree or show frustration with one another in front of children. But children learn how to resolve conflicts in their own relationships by watching other people resolve *their* conflicts.

Think about how you handle conflicts. Try to model an assertive approach that implies, and may even explicitly state, that:

- You have a right to disagree, but that you think a compromise can be reached.
- You respect the other person's point of view even though you may not share it.
- You have a right to make requests and to express your feelings but not to put another person down or to call him names or make blaming statements. Requests that meet this description are called "I statements" because they begin with "I" rather than "you." An example might be, "I get upset when you [leave your clothes on the bathroom floor] because [it makes the bathroom look really messy]. I would like you to [pick up your clothes when you leave the bathroom]." Compare that to the more common approach: "How many times have I told you to pick your clothes up off the bathroom floor? I can't believe what a slob you are."

Name-calling, blaming statements, and put-downs fuel the child's inner inflamer voice. In conflict situations, the child is likely to say to himself things similar to what you have said to him. The resulting anger will get in the way of his being able to resolve the conflict.

Affirmations

Before a child negotiates or tries to handle conflict, he can repeat to himself:

"I deserve to say what I feel."
"I am a worthwhile person with worthwhile ideas and valid opinions."
"I am strong and can handle disagreements."

As with the other affirmations listed in this chapter, the younger the child, the simpler, and sometimes more general, the affirmation will need to be. For instance, a five-year-old would probably do better with "I can stand up for myself" than "I can say what I believe even if others don't agree."

Remember that affirmations are most effective when they are stated in the child's words, reflect the child's goals, and are repeated frequently and in conflict-free situations. Once a child is *in* a conflict, other strategies are needed.

Challenging negative self-talk

Although assertiveness is not generally thought to be an important characteristic for children to develop, it is. Unassertive children—either passive or aggressive—don't handle conflict well. The passive child is easily taken advantage of. He doesn't stand up for his rights and usually solves conflicts by giving in. He typically says things—to himself or out loud—such as:

> "What can I do? I asked for my toy and he wouldn't give it back."
> "I don't really want to do that, but if I tell them, they won't like me anymore."
> "It won't do any good to talk about it. She never listens to me."

The aggressive child has the opposite problem. He pushes others around. People often describe him as bossy or demanding because he assumes that he should always get his way. He handles conflicts by trying to make other people do what he wants, and he usually gets angry when they don't comply. His speech is riddled with gimme's, no's, and I don't want to's. For example, he might be heard saying:

> "Stop that. I don't want to do it that way."
> "I should get to be first."
> "I said be quiet. It's my turn."

Both passive and aggressive children need to understand and remind themselves about the principles of assertiveness mentioned above in the discussion of modeling. They need to remember that they (and others) have a right to express their feelings, disagree, and make requests, but that no one has the right to put others down or call them names. The exact words they use to remind themselves of these principles will depend on the nature of their negative self-talk and their age.

Here are some examples of self-talk that challenges the passive and aggressive statements above:

> "I need to have my toys back when I ask for them. I'll have to think of something else to do if this doesn't work."
>
> "I can make decisions about what I want to do and what I don't want to do. I don't always have to do what others want to keep them as friends."
>
> "It may not work out to talk about this problem, but I need to try. I don't have to agree with her just because she's my friend. Besides, if I don't tell her how I feel [or what I want], how can I expect her to know?"
>
> "People don't have to do things my way all the time. Maybe if I do it his way this time, he'll do it my way next time."
>
> "Everyone wants to be first. It's hard, but I can learn to take turns."
>
> "People get excited when we do group work. Just because someone interrupts me doesn't mean he's mean or rude. I just have to remind him and ask him nicely to wait his turn. Maybe if I can remember to be quiet during his turn, he'll do the same for me."

PRACTICING

As with anything else, social skills develop with practice. Practice may not make perfect, but it certainly makes better. You can provide the child with practice by presenting hypothetical social situations, reading books, playing games, and rehearsing or role-playing. If the child gets positive feedback and sees improvement in his social skills in these safe settings, he will feel more confident and be better able to handle real-life social interaction.

HYPOTHETICAL SITUATIONS

Asking a child what he thinks about hypothetical situations is a nonthreatening way to extend his thinking and to encourage him to talk about the way he perceives events in his own life.

Here are some hypothetical situations you could discuss with five- to ten-year-olds.

Trying to make friends

You might say, "Tell me what you would do in this case. April is new to the school and wants to make friends. She sees three girls her age talking to each other at lunch. What should she do to try to make friends with them? What might she say to them? What might April be saying to herself? What could she say that would make herself feel brave enough to go up to them?"

Coping with rejection, disapproval, or social failure

You might say, "Bradley wanted to join his classmates who were playing dodgeball at lunchtime. One of them said no. Bradley went away and didn't play the rest of the period. What do you think Bradley was saying to himself about not being able to play? What could he have said to himself to have a better time? What could he have done differently?"

A conflict situation that calls for negotiation and self-control

You might say, "June was standing in line with her classmates when someone pushed her. June started crying. She felt so embarrassed about crying in front of everyone that she had to leave the line and go into the bathroom. What do you think June said to herself about being pushed that made her cry? What might she have said to herself that could have helped her to handle the situation differently?"

Hypothetical situations also present wonderful opportunities for bringing up, in an indirect way, specific problems that you may have observed in the child's social interactions, or irrational ideas you feel she may have. For example, you might ask if the child thinks that the girl in the story believes that she's bad or there's something wrong with her because she wasn't included. Introducing irrational ideas through other people can allow the child to think about them objectively.

BOOKS

Another way to help children think about social situations and talk about them in productive ways is to read books together. Many children's books detail the struggle of trying to relate to friends in positive and empathetic ways. Asking questions about a story, as you did with hypothetical situations, can help a child to expand his undertanding of social situations.

GAMES

Games are another nonthreatening way to expand a child's understanding of social situations. "The Talking, Feeling, and Doing Game" is a commercially produced board game that is noncompetitive and fun for children and parents to play together. You could expand the game fairly easily to include questions about what people were saying to themselves.

A game that is lots of fun to play while driving is "What Would You Say to Yourself?" Start by giving the child a hypothetical situation. For example, "Your best friend just walked by you without even looking at you or saying anything." Then ask him, "What would you say to yourself? How would what you said to yourself make you feel?" Be sure to accept whatever answers he gives without correcting or judging him. Then have him try you out on a hypothetical situation in return. You'll be amazed at how quickly the child will see the relationship between what he says to himself and how he feels.

ROLE-PLAYING AND REHEARSING

Just talking about what a child might say to himself in a social setting and how he might approach another person is helpful, but it often isn't enough. People who are afraid of rejection or confrontation tend to avoid getting involved in encounters that may lead to either one.

The same is true in other circumstances, social or not: A

child is unlikely to put herself in a situation that she thinks will be difficult for her, so she isn't getting any practice in handling it. Without practice, her skills won't increase.

When you have a child rehearse ahead of time what she will say—both to herself and out loud—she will be less fearful and will feel more self-confident when the actual situation arises. Furthermore, if you give encouragement and positive feedback, she will repeat those statements to herself and they will give her strength to meet new social challenges.

Depending on the child's skills, you may need to make very specific suggestions about what she should do. You can encourage the child to repeat those instructions to herself once the encounter occurs. For example, you might suggest that she tell herself when initiating contact with others, "Remember to smile and to speak so other people can hear me. I also need to remember that the other person's response is not a reflection of the kind of person I am. I *want* the other person to respond positively, but I don't *have* to have that."

It is often helpful when role-playing or rehearsing to repeat the practice several times. Be careful, however, to give honest, positive feedback along with suggestions for improvement.

CONCLUSION

This chapter shouldn't imply that making changes in self-talk brings about magical changes in behavior. Learning how to relate to others is a long process. But if we can encourage the supportive voices that help children to act in positive ways, they will feel more up to the task of learning how to relate to others.

Changing self-talk about any issue isn't a one-time proposition. You can't expect one discussion about positive self-talk to work a miracle. You need to establish an atmosphere of openness that makes talking about relationships feel safe, and then help children explore new ways of doing things.

Even though changing a child's self-talk takes time, studies have shown that it is one of the quickest ways to change social behavior. So be patient and congratulate yourself for applying these steps to the area of friendships. Guiding your child's acquisition of social skills is a worthwhile investment in helping him toward a happy and harmonious life.

· 9 ·

FRIENDSHIPS IN LATE CHILDHOOD AND ADOLESCENCE

* * *

All I really want in life is to be normal.
—*Anonymous*

By the time children enter their teens, they have learned how to handle friendships with a bit more tact than in earlier years. The rejections are more subtle—"My mom says I can have only one person over at a time" instead of "I don't like you anymore. Amy's my best friend now"—and the interactions in general seem less primitive. Most children have mastered the basic relationship skills discussed in the last chapter. They can identify and label their own feelings; they can understand how other people might feel in a given situation (that is, they can empathize); and they can understand the effects of their own behavior on others. Most can solve relatively complex social problems because they now understand cause and effect and can generate solutions and think about probable consequences much better than they could when they were younger.

Why, then, do they seem to have so many social problems? At times, it seems that they have *fewer* skills in forming and maintaining friendships than do their younger cohorts. Many still have trouble initiating contact with other people, and if someone approaches them, they withdraw and become self-conscious. Most, at one time or another, are overly sensitive about rejection and disapproval. A simple suggestion is taken as a personal attack; an unreturned phone call is proof that a friend doesn't like them anymore. And conflicts abound. There may be weeks on end when "best friends" don't talk to one another because of an unresolved argument, or when phone calls end in harsh words or tears.

Seeing a teenager or a preteen having these kinds of friendship problems, one might wonder if she learned *anything* in the first ten years of her life about how to get along. Unless adults understand the developmental tasks and milestones of this age group, they are apt to be confused, frustrated, and even angry about the way teenagers act. But a sense of what children of this age are dealing with—emotionally, cognitively, physically, and socially—can provide patience and compassion, two essential characteristics if parents are to help them to have more satisfying relationships.

DEVELOPMENTAL TASKS AND MILESTONES

Physical development occurs more rapidly in early adolescence than at any other time in life except infancy. Maybe you can remember some of the physical changes you and your peers experienced in your pre- or early teen years: Growth spurts were common, but happened at different times for different people, so that suddenly some girls towered several inches over boys the same age. Sexual development also occurred at different rates, so that some of your friends looked like adults, others like children. Some of the boys developed "peach fuzz" on their faces and their voices changed—though not all at once, so that they would crack without warning in mid-sentence. Some of the girls began to develop curves and breasts. Waiting for their menstrual periods to begin was traumatic. No one wanted to be the first to have it happen, but no one wanted to be the last, either.

As an adult, you know that some of the physical changes that occur in adolescence are lasting and some are temporary. Acne and that gangly awkwardness that assails some adolescents when they haven't yet become used to their "new" bodies are examples of troublesome but temporary conditions. For the young person experiencing them, they are especially worrisome. He feels as if he will never again have clear skin or be able to walk without stumbling over his own feet.

Unlike the physical changes of adolescence, the intellectual changes are all permanent and are almost always experienced as positive. Some scientists believe the brain actually grows larger at this time. A child's memory improves dramatically in early adolescence. Even more important is the development of abstract thinking. Teenagers can "think in their heads"—that is, consider things and situations they can't see or aren't immediately experiencing. They can also make comparisons between different points of view. Because of these cognitive developments, they become better problem solvers: They can analyze and critique literature, figure out difficult math problems, and hypothesize about the results of a science experiment. When other issues don't interfere, they can also solve social problems more easily than they could when they were younger and able to engage only in concrete thinking.

Especially relevant to forming and maintaining friendships are the changes in social roles that take place in adolescence. As young people move out of childhood and into adulthood, their relationships with one another and adults change dramatically. Acceptance by peers becomes more critical than ever, in part because of the adolescent's need to become more independent of her parents and to form a separate identity. Adolescents tend to look to one another instead of their parents for clues as to what that identity might be, and they often "try on" several roles before they settle on a particular set of values and beliefs. It is ironic that their need to be independent from adult authority encourages them to conform blindly to peer expectations and norms. For a while, a teenager may seem less independent and able to think for himself than an eight-year-old! But this searching and the need to be accepted by peers are necessary preludes to developing autonomy and a strong sense of self.

Not only do they feel even greater pressure to be accepted by peers, teens also have a whole new social arena to learn about and master—that of dating and relating to members of the opposite sex. Suddenly they must face new situations that call for new skills: how to ask someone out; how to show an interest and *encourage* someone to ask you out; how to let someone know you *aren't* interested; how to say no to sex, drinking, or drugs without seeming too straight or uptight. Even youngsters in same-sex relationships will now often find themselves nervous, self-conscious, and at a loss to know how to deal with these new demands.

All of these rapid physical, intellectual, and social changes take an emotional toll on the emerging young adult. Her emotions run the gamut from ecstasy to deepest depression. At any given moment she might feel isolated, unloved and misunderstood, confused, scared, angry, or self-conscious and embarrassed. Entering the teen years is like being on a roller coaster—with one important difference: The teen can slow down and straighten out some of the curves by learning how to use positive self-talk so the ride isn't quite so harrowing.

THE ROLE OF SELF-TALK

Laura is a junior in high school and has never been on a date. She is shy and self-conscious around boys but seems quite at ease with girls. Laura sees herself as unattractive and says things to herself like, "He'd never go for me. I'm just not pretty enough," or "I don't know what to say. He's going to think I'm boring." As a consequence, she never responds to boys' overtures because she assumes that there's some mistake ("I just *think* he's smiling at me," for instance), they have ulterior motives ("He really likes my girlfriend and is just trying to make her jealous"), or they wouldn't really like her if they got to know her.

Unlike Laura, fourteen-year-old Julie's problems center around her girlfriends rather than around boys. She feels used because they make plans with her and then break the plans if something better comes along at the last minute. Although she's crying as often as not when she gets off the phone with one of them, she feels helpless to do anything about the situation because she is afraid that if she gets angry or says anything, they won't like her anymore.

Twelve-year-old Justin has problems handling peer pressure. Like Julie, he's afraid that if he says no or doesn't go along with what his friends want to do, they won't be his friends anymore. They don't take advantage of him or treat him inconsiderately the way Julie's friends treat her. It wouldn't even be fair to say that they exert *direct* pressure on him to cut class, smoke, or drink when they do. But Justin *feels* the pressure. He wants so badly to be part of the group that he does things he knows are wrong, things he really doesn't want to do.

These three young people could have more satisfying relationships if they learned new forms of self-talk.

Laura could remind herself that she'll never get comfortable around boys if she doesn't spend time with them. She might learn to make positive affirmations to herself, like, "I am an attractive girl and boys like me," or "I am as comfortable around boys as I am around my girlfriends." Laura also needs to learn how to show interest and approach boys. By role-playing and learning to instruct herself through the steps involved in initiating contact with a boy, she would gain self-confidence as well as skill.

Julie needs to know that she has the right to express her dismay to her friends and to request that they behave differently. She needs to rehearse in her mind what she wants to say. She would probably benefit from reminding herself, before she confronts a friend, that "I need to know ahead of time what I'm going to be doing, and my friends can't be expected to know how I feel if I don't tell them."

Similarly, Justin needs to practice saying no and rehearsing or role-playing how to handle it when his friends want him to join them in doing something he doesn't want to do. Reminding himself of the possible consequences of cutting class, smoking, or drinking may help give him the courage to say no. He might also think about friendships and how he would feel if the tables were turned. For example, he might say to himself, "Real friends don't care if you drink or smoke as long as you don't lay a trip on *them* for doing it. I wouldn't pressure a friend to do something he didn't want to do, and I'm sure my friends would treat me with the same respect. If they don't, they're not really my friends."

Your child may not have social problems as pronounced as these, but she can probably use some help in learning to talk to herself in positive ways. Changing her self-talk can make her relationships more satisfying.

Before we discuss how to help children between the ages of eleven and eighteen use self-talk to improve their friendships, let's look at what happens to adult-child relationships at this time.

ADULT-CHILD RELATIONSHIPS DURING THE TEEN YEARS

"That's unfair. You treat me like a baby."
"You don't trust me."
"You just don't understand."
"I hate you."
"You don't let me do *anything*. Everybody else gets to go."

Almost every parent of a teenager or preteen has heard at least some of these complaints more than once. Even youngsters who previously were respectful, compliant, and well-mannered may become disrespectful, rebellious, and rude to their elders when they enter the teen years.

One of the developmental tasks of adolescence is to separate or "individuate" from one's parents and begin to form one's own identity, a difficult and often painful process for all concerned. It requires that the child reject, or at least question, many of the values and beliefs he has been taught, that he begin to assert himself in the adult world, that he take on new responsibilities and make more independent decisions. Furthermore, it requires that he experience the *consequences* of those decisions, because by doing so he will really find out how the adult world works.

But parents all know how traumatic those consequences can be. Standing by and letting their child suffer negative consequences goes against their natural inclination to protect him. Even when they know intellectually that "that's how he'll learn," their instinct to protect may be so overpowering that they rush in and rescue the child from an irate teacher, a failing grade, or an embarrassing situation. In part, this happens because parents remember the painful lessons they themselves learned, and they hope their child can learn without having to experience the same pain.

Another reason this is a difficult time for parents is that they are so devalued. Again, they may know intellectually that their child needs to denigrate them or at least question their authority in order to become a separate, independent adult, but still it is very disturbing to be the object of scorn and abuse after years of selfless love and sacrifice. Parents often respond in very human ways—with anger, resentment, or withdrawal.

For their part, children respond to their parents with ambivalence, at best, during this trying period. They are angry that they aren't given more freedom or treated in a more adult fashion, though they often don't want the responsibility that goes with freedom. They resent the limits parents put on them, but will push for limits and get even angrier if they aren't forthcoming. They complain that "nobody understands" but they withdraw to their rooms for hours or days at a time and never tell anyone what is going on, so how *can* you understand? They may ask for advice but are likely to ignore it.

It seems that parents—and to a lesser degree, other adults—are in a no-win situation. Even if they know how to help a child with a particular problem, they question whether their input will be accepted.

But when parents and other adults can let go of the urge to fix all the child's problems or to save him from pain, they can be more objective and therefore more helpful to him. Self-talk can be a useful tool toward that end. For instance, you might remind yourself, "This is *his* problem, not mine," or "I can't solve it for him, but I can listen and make suggestions; the rest is up to him."

Parents of teenagers need to redefine their own roles. Once a parent can acknowledge that a particular problem is the child's and not his, as is the case with forming and maintaining friendships, the parent needs to become less of an authority figure and more of a friend and confidant. Instead of "I think you should do such-and-such," he needs to say, "Have you ever thought of . . . ?" or "I have a similar problem. What I find works for me is . . ." Putting the ball back in the child's court like this is usually more effective at *any* age than telling her what to do, but it is an especially critical skill when working with teenagers because of their need to exert their independence.

The examples in the next section illustrate how parents and other adults can help adolescents with relationship problems *in spite of* the ambivalence and tension inherent in adult-child relationships at this age.

USING POSITIVE SELF-TALK IN SOCIAL SITUATIONS

MODELING

Modeling how to initiate a friendship or solve conflicts in the presence of a teen or preteen is just as helpful as it is with younger children. Telling the child about what you say to yourself to help you through these situations is also important. Although you can't stage being disapproved of or rejected just so you can demonstrate how to handle rejection, when it happens in the normal course of events, as it does for everyone, you can share your self-talk with the young person.

Modeling how to handle dating and opposite-sex relationships is a little different. As an adult, even if you are single, your opposite-sex relationships differ considerably from what they were when you were a teenager. You probably feel much more confident and clearer about what you want, and you probably have less difficulty saying no. Because you are no longer a novice in handling opposite-sex relationships, and in fact may not even be dating, you need to model how to do it by telling the child what you remember about how you dealt with it when you were his age.

For instance, to his son who is afraid to ask a girl out, a father might say, "I remember being terrified to call girls on the phone. The only thing that finally worked was to talk to myself. I'd practice exactly what I wanted to say and give myself a little pep talk before picking up the phone. I'd say things like, 'Maybe she'll say yes, and maybe she won't, but I know she's interested, so even if she can't go, she's not going to be rude. I'll just ask another time.' "

To a girl who is feeling pressured to have sex with her boyfriend, a mother might say, "I dated a guy in high school like that. I really liked him and almost gave in, but I kept telling myself that if he broke up with me just because I wouldn't go all the way, he couldn't really care for me much. He *did* break up with me and for a while I thought I'd really blown it. But when he got another girl pregnant and then broke up with her, too, I knew I'd made the right decision."

Another way to use modeling to help teenagers with social problems of all kinds is to have them think about how one of their heroes might handle a situation. Junior high kids look up to high school kids, high school kids look up to college kids, and almost all teens have heroes who are sports figures, movie stars, or musicians. If you know something about your youngster's hero and are fairly sure he is a positive example, you might ask, "How would [the name of the hero] handle this situation? What do you think he'd say to himself to get up the courage to go against what his friends wanted?"

AFFIRMATIONS

As with younger children, teenagers can use affirmations to reprogram themselves to have more successful relationships. Repeating affirmations upon first awakening, when going to bed, and before they get into difficult situations can sometimes prevent negative self-talk.

Many of the examples of affirmations given in the last chapter would be appropriate for teenagers as well as for younger children. For example:

"I am an attractive, likable person."
"I can meet new people."

"I like getting to know people, and people like getting to know me."
"I remember how to make conversation and let someone know I am interested in them."
"I can deal with whatever comes my way."
"I deserve to say what I feel."
"I am a worthwhile person with worthwhile ideas and valid opinions."
"I am strong and can handle disagreements."

In addition, older children *might* practice, in their own wording, affirmations that are more complex conceptually, are less vague, and/or focus more on concerns that are especially relevant to this age. For example:

"I am a strong, independent thinker. I can make up my own mind regardless of what my friends think."
"Boys [or girls] like me."
"I'm a good conversationalist. I have interesting things to say and I'm funny."
"I am a good problem solver."
"People don't have to agree with me. I don't have to agree with others. I can handle differences of opinion."
"I can say no without losing my friends."

CHALLENGING NEGATIVE SELF-TALK

With teenagers as with younger children, an effective challenge to negative self-talk helps put the situation in perspective. It corrects distorted ways of thinking like overgeneralizing

("*Everybody* is going,") and catastrophizing ("It will be terrible if I don't have a date. I'll die") and it minimizes "What if's" ("What if he doesn't like me anymore?" "What if she doesn't invite me to her party?" "What if they ignore me?"). It also helps the youngster overcome the sense that each interaction is a make-or-break situation.

Because of their greater ability to think abstractly, adolescents can learn to ask themselves a series of questions that guide them through disputing their own negative self-talk. This is a more desirable approach than suggesting specific things they could say to themselves because it gives them more autonomy. They are less likely to say, "You don't understand," or "That's stupid. That would never work," if you aren't telling them what to say.

Here are questions that an adolescent can ask himself when he catches himself engaged in negative self-talk:

1. What evidence is there that this statement is true?
2. What evidence is there that this statement is false?
3. What is the worst thing that could happen to me if what I want to happen doesn't, or what I don't want to happen does?
4. What good things might occur if what I want to happen doesn't or what I don't want to happen does?

Let's use Justin (whom we introduced at the beginning of this chapter) to illustrate this process.

When Justin told his counselor, "If I hadn't cut English with them and they'd been caught, they would have thought I ratted on them and then they wouldn't be my friends anymore," she asked him to examine that statement more carefully. Together, they went through each of the above questions and Justin came up with the following conclusions:

1. "Well, Brad accused Joe of ratting on them when he didn't cut math with them a couple weeks ago and they got caught."
2. "No one else blamed Joe, and even Brad decided later that he'd been wrong. He even apologized to Joe, and I think he likes Joe more now than before."
3. "Realistically, the worst thing that would happen if I didn't cut with them is that they might be a little bent out of shape at me for a while. If I *did* cut, the worst thing that could happen would be that I'd get suspended and my grade would go down."
4. "If I didn't cut, it might give some of the other guys the guts to stand up to Brad, too. I don't think most of them really want to cut. They're just afraid to cross Brad. I think they might respect me more, too."

By keeping the discussion light, not preaching, and not telling Justin what to do, Justin's counselor was able to help him see that his thinking was irrational. He felt relieved to have concluded that he might actually *improve* his standing with his friends by not cutting class with them. As important, Justin felt that he solved this problem himself. Because he felt successful and empowered by the process, he used it more and more often, and it eventually became almost automatic.

Here are some examples of negative self-talk related to friendships that teenagers often engage in. You might practice asking yourself the four questions listed on page 165 about each statement. If your conclusion challenges the negative comment and puts the situation in perspective, you are ready to help a teenager learn how to challenge his own negative self-talk.

"I just don't fit in. Nobody likes me."
"I'll just get all nervous and make a fool of myself if I try to talk to him. What's the use?"
"I have to go along with the crowd or no one will like me."
"I know she won't go to the dance with me. Why ask?"

SELF-INSTRUCTION

When a teenager's social problems stem in part from his not knowing what to say or do in a given situation, modeling, affirmations, and challenges may not be enough. He also needs to learn how to instruct himself—to talk himself through each step and encourage himself as he goes along.

You can teach a teenager to instruct herself through the stages of a difficult social situation. First, demonstrate instructing yourself by saying each step out loud to yourself as you perform it. Second, have the adolescent practice doing the same thing. Finally, have her go through each step while instructing herself silently.

With enough practice, when she gets into real-life social situations that are difficult for her, she will know how to talk herself through them. Eventually, her self-instruction will become so automatic that she won't even be aware of doing it.

When they moved, Sharon's mother helped her learn how to instruct herself in meeting new people. This is what Sharon learned to do:

When she saw someone on her street or on the playground

whom she wanted to meet, she would say to herself, "Okay, here's my chance. Just stay calm. First, I have to walk over closer and keep looking at them, and remember to smile while I walk." (She starts walking, checking herself to be sure she's following her own instructions.) "Good. Okay, I'm almost close enough to say hi. I have to remember to speak up and tell them my name before I ask them theirs." (She introduces herself, watches and listens for their response, notes how she's doing.) "Good. Okay, now I'll ask them if I can play."

ROLE-PLAYING AND REHEARSING

Being able to practice a new behavior in a safe environment where you know no one will laugh at you and where you can get honest feedback on your performance is an important part of acquiring a new skill at any age. Again, practice may not make perfect, but it certainly makes better.

The more complex the skill, the more important practice is. Friendship-making skills are *very* complex, but teenagers are usually too self-conscious to practice in front of peers. An adult who knows how to use positive self-talk in his own relationships and who understands how to relate to teenagers is the perfect candidate for guiding an adolescent's practice.

The nature of the practice depends on the nature of the problem. Young people who know what to do and say in a social situation, but who say such negative things to themselves that they cannot perform, need *covert* practice. That is, they need to practice changing what they say in their heads rather than what they say out loud. This kind of practice, called rehearsal or mental rehearsal, can be done alone, but it is usually helpful if an adult demonstrates.

For example, a child who knows how to say no without being mean or insulting, but who has trouble doing so because she is afraid people won't like her, might benefit from having an adult share what he says to himself when he has to say no to someone ("I remind myself that I have a right to say no and that it's my responsibility to take care of myself"). The youngster can then formulate her own internal dialogue and rehearse it.

More commonly, the youngster engages in negative self-talk *and* needs practice carrying out the overt behavior. Such is usually the case when shyness or fear of rejection is involved. The child fears rejection because he is saying something to himself like, "I don't know what to say," or "He isn't interested in me," or "No one likes me," and, because he avoids making contact with others, his friendship-making skills are rusty, too. In his mind, he needs to rehearse or self-instruct how to make contact with another person, but he also needs to actually practice *doing* it. Role-playing is an effective way to give him that practice in a safe environment where he can get encouragement and constructive feedback.

It is often most useful for the adult to play the youngster's part first in order to demonstrate the appropriate behavior. Covert behavior can be demonstrated at the same time as overt behavior by "thinking out loud." Then the youngster can take over his own part and role-play the situation several times. You must be careful to provide balanced feedback—honest, positive feedback, along with suggestions for improvement.

PUTTING IT ALL TOGETHER

Role-playing, rehearsing, and self-instruction are usually used in conjunction with the other techniques discussed in this chapter. To show how a parent or adult might put all this together, let's go back to Laura and Julie, whom we introduced earlier.

Laura really wanted to go to her junior prom but no one had asked her. Her mother urged her to ask a friend from school. She realistically pointed out that while the boy might say no, he might be too shy to ask anyone and would feel flattered to be invited. "If he does say he can't go, I'm sure he will do it in a nice way, and you won't be any worse off than you are now," her mother told her.

Then her mom talked about ways she might approach the phone call. "Just tell yourself that he'll be really happy to hear from you, and that asking him will make him feel good about himself. Keep telling yourself how brave you are and what a liberated woman you are to be asking a man out." She also discussed how Laura could use self-instruction: She could prepare for the call by instructing herself about each step ahead of time ("First I'll ask about school. Then I'll ask if he's already going to the dance . . ."), and during the call, she could tell herself what to do next, check to make sure she was doing it, and then encourage herself silently.

Laura's mother knew that people who are good at initiating relationships don't invest a lot in the outcome of each overture. They have a "win some, lose some" attitude and don't view rejection as a tragedy. She communicated this understanding by saying that even if the boy said no, he would still be flattered and would probably decline in a nice way.

Julie's mother knew that Julie needed to be able to set limits with her friends but that before she could tell her friends what she wanted and didn't want, she first had to know what that was. People like Julie tend to be so concerned with what others think that they lose touch with what they themselves want. Julie's mother helped her by asking, "What do you want to say to Trixie? What do you want your friends to do in this situation?"

By sharing her own experiences with self-talk, Julie's mom helped her learn to remind herself that she was worthy of respect and that she didn't want to be dropped by people at the last minute. Julie would say things to herself like, "I need to know what I'm going to be doing ahead of time. I don't have to blame anyone, but I need to let her know my feelings about the situation. Maybe she just doesn't know how I feel. If she continues to break dates at the last minute, maybe I won't make plans with her next time."

These statements would give her courage to call her friend back and let her know how she felt. But negotiating with other people is tricky. When one is first learning to speak up for oneself, it's important to rehearse alone or with another person what one wants to say. Julie and her mom role-played and Julie practiced her message to her friend.

CONCLUSION

Many of the social problems of older children and adolescents are developmental. Even though they are more advanced cognitively than their younger cohorts, the rapid physical, intellectual, and social changes they undergo take an emotional toll. New demands—like having to grow more independent of their parents and beginning to date and form relationships with the opposite sex—keep them from behaving in as considerate or harmonious a manner as their years and intellectual development might suggest they should.

Although emotional upheaval is inherent in adolescence,

learning to talk positively to oneself can reduce the stress and trauma of friendships during this time. Modeling, affirmations, and challenging self-talk are as effective toward this end as they are with younger children. Similarly, practice is as important in the area of adolescents' friendships as it is with a child of any age who is trying to learn any new skill. The more complex strategies like role-playing, mental rehearsal, and self-instruction can help the adolescent practice new ways to approach new social challenges with confidence and a positive attitude.

· 10 ·
SELF-TALK AND HEALTH

PROGRAMMING CHILDREN FOR HEALTH

• • •

The greatest force in the human body is the natural drive of the body to heal itself—but that force is not independent of the belief system, which can translate expectations into physiological change. Nothing is more wondrous about the fifteen billion neurons in the human brain than their ability to convert thoughts, hopes, ideas, and attitudes into chemical substances. Everything begins, therefore, with belief. What we believe is the most powerful option of all.

—*Norman Cousins*

In the past, scientists were sure that disease was caused by germs. But today we know that the belief system of the person is a major determinant in his susceptibility to illness.

Bernie S. Siegel is one of the many doctors exploring the healing potential of the mind. In 1978 he founded Exceptional Cancer Patients, a therapy program that promotes physical healing through personal change. Siegel, the author of *Love, Medicine, and Miracles*, is interested in the effect that emotions and thoughts have on brain and body chemicals. In his book he says the following:

> Consider some of our common expressions: "He is a pain in the neck." "Get off my back." "This problem is eating me alive." "You're breaking my heart." The body responds to the mind's messages. I am convinced we have not only survival mechanisms, such as the flight or fight response, but also "die" mechanisms, which actively stop our defenses, slow our bodies' functions, and bring us toward death when we feel our lives are not worth living.
>
> We don't yet understand all the ways in which brain chemicals are related to emotions and thoughts, but the salient point is that our state of mind has an immediate and direct effect on the state of our body. We can change the body by dealing with how we feel. If we ignore our despair, the body receives a "die" message. If we deal with our pain and seek help, then the message is, *Living is difficult but desirable*, and the immune system works to keep us alive.

Most of us don't think of health in terms of "live" or "die" messages, but being aware of the potential effects of self-statements on our immune systems and general health is the first step toward changing those messages.

Much of the current thinking about health attitudes centers around the role of stress and its relation to health. Stress has been identified as the culprit in many minor illnesses and serious diseases, from the common cold to heart disease. But unfortunately, this is only part of the story. It is one's attitude toward stressful events that affects one's health, not the events themselves.

THE RELATIONSHIP BETWEEN SELF-TALK, ATTITUDES, AND HEALTH

Patterns for handling disturbing situations are formed in early childhood, when people first develop self-talk and learn to interpret events in their lives in particular ways. Unfortunately, adults are often unaware of the attitudes toward tension that a child is developing.

It is known that stress and change are directly related to illnesses in children, as they are in adults. Children who experience stressful events are twice as likely to become ill as children who do not. This suggests that children need to be equipped with attitudes that can help them maintain health and resiliency even in the face of anxiety.

A study by Dr. Albert Siebert revealed that people who had undergone high levels of stress and came out emotionally and physically on top had specific common characteristics. One of those characteristics was the ability to have positive conversations with themselves.

One of the most important factors in health is one's attitude: one's vision of one's individual health and the belief that one can carry out health goals. Self-talk is one of the crucial determinants of attitude.

In order to program our children and ourselves for health we have to learn health-giving outlooks. We need to replace old priorities with those validated by recent scientific research. Here are some surprising findings that can help you understand how attitudes affect health.

1. *Laughing is important for good health.* ("Lighten up and have some fun, it's good for you.")

    Laughter activates the immune system and creates an

anabolic state—the state opposite to stress. Laughter increases muscle activity and the flow of oxygen to the bloodstream and raises the body temperature. A doctor in Tokyo has reported success in using laughter to combat TB.

As one observer of its effects noted: "Laughter is one of the best medicines. . . . It is a form of internal jogging. It moves your internal organs around. It enhances respiration. It is an igniter of great expectations."

One of the most famous cases of self-healing through laughter is documented by Norman Cousins in *Anatomy of an Illness*. Cousins used comedy films to help him recover from a potentially fatal disease. Doctors noted that his rate of infection improved after each screening of comedy films.

2. *Crying reduces stress-related diseases.* ("It's okay to cry. You'll feel better if you get it out.")

   Research shows that the more crying a person does, the less likely he is to suffer from a stress-related disease. A 1979 study by two doctors, Walter Smith and Stephen Bloomfield, concluded that people who cry frequently have fewer colds. When scientists analyzed tears shed by people who were emotionally upset, they found that they contained protein, unlike the tears caused by peeling an onion or by smog. Tears remove chemicals that build up in stressful situations and they have been shown to relieve headaches, calm nerves, and reduce blood pressure.

3. *Feeling a sense of self-efficacy and control helps us maintain health and even reduces pain.* ("I know I can influence what happens to me and how I feel"; "I'm not helpless.")

   Extreme cases of depression have been successfully

treated without medication by helping the patients see that how they think affects their feelings. Many adult and childhood illnesses are associated with feeling a lack of control in one's life. Research shows that when people feel helpless, they are more apt to become ill.

4. *Reaching out to friends and family in positive ways contributes to health.* ("I need a hug"; "I'm feeling kind of down. I think I'll call Dottie and see if she wants to go to a movie or something"; "I really don't want to socialize, but I know I'll feel better if I go to the party.")

Scientists are now convinced that social support is one of the most important contributing factors to human health. People without friends are more likely to become ill and have a higher rate of mortality as a result of their diseases than people who have the support of family and friends. Conversely, social support reduces stress and enhances people's abilities to resist and recover from disease. It has been shown to affect a person's immune system, his psychological state, and the length of his life.

Support has been related to recovery in a variety of illnesses, from arthritis to TB, not to mention alcoholism, depression, and other psychiatric illnesses. Support can also reduce the amount of medication a person needs.

5. *Having positive interests in life helps us to thrive.* ("Just sitting around and watching TV isn't good for me. I think I'll take up biking.")

In *Getting Well Again* Carl and Stephanie Simonton tell of two men who reacted in different ways when told they had the same life-threatening illness. One man stopped working almost from the day he got the diagnosis and went home and watched TV all day. He gave up all the things he liked to do, such as fishing. He died in a short time.

The other man continued to work every day, even while he was receiving treatment. When he learned of the disease, he realized that many things in his life had lost meaning for him. As a result, he started to spend more time with his family, even having them accompany him on business trips. One day he said, "You know, I had forgotten that I hadn't looked at the trees and the grass and the flowers for a long time, and now I do that." This man survived much longer and enjoyed his life more.

Being healthy doesn't mean that you will never get sick. If health is defined as balance or harmony between different parts, then it's easy to see that active engagement in life can keep people healthy even if they are sick. That seems like a contradiction in terms, but as Dr. Kenneth Pelletier points out, even someone with cancer or another catastrophic illness can lead a healthy life by pursuing interests that he loves and remaining engaged in the world around him. Feeling involved and alive is essential to programming oneself for good health.

DEVELOPMENTAL ISSUES

Health is sometimes less important to children than to adults because they haven't lived long enough to appreciate it. It also changes in importance as children develop. One study found that health concerns were common among elementary-school children, whereas social and psychological concerns became more important in junior and senior high. But regardless of the child's natural developmental concerns, when adults talk about health as something that is affected by self-talk and attitudes, children are often fascinated. Learning to work with concepts like these at a young age can help a child have healthy viewpoints and habits for the rest of his life.

CHILDHOOD PROBLEMS AND HEALTH

These findings can help adults understand some approaches to children's health and some of the problems they experience. Here are some common ways that difficulties and negative self-talk are related to childhood illnesses, according to research and professional observation:

1. *Chronic flu and colds* are often related to stress in children, especially when they feel helpless and unable to affect their lives in positive ways. Such children may be saying to themselves, "I can't handle this"; "Nothing ever goes right for me"; "It doesn't matter how hard I try, it won't do any good"; "Nobody ever listens to me."
2. *Wetting and soiling* after a child has been toilet-trained can occur when a child has a sense that he is helpless and out of control. These maladies are also sometimes symptoms of anger. Children who wet and soil may say things like, "I'll show him"; "This will get her attention"; "I can't help it."
3. *Anorexia and bulimia* are eating disorders that have come to public attention in recent years. Anorexia, an extreme re-

sistance to proper eating, can result in life-threatening weight loss and sometimes even death. Bulimia is bingeing on food and then vomiting. Both of these eating disorders are related to issues of control. Most of the victims of these disorders are girls who have perfectionist attitudes and an obsessive fear of loss of control in their lives. Their self-talk is probably something like, "I have to be thin"; "I have to have a beautiful figure or no one will like me"; "If I gain a pound, it means I'm losing control and I'll get fat."

4. *Chronic stomachaches, ulcers, and colitis* in children and young people can all spring from a feeling of helplessness in handling tension and stress and the tendency to turn fear and anxiety inward. These illnesses are typically forms of inner aggressiveness and taking anger out on oneself. Children who suffer from these conditions usually say things to themselves like, "It's all my fault"; "I'm a bad person"; "No one likes me."

5. *Headaches* are another stress-related illness that occurs when children feel helpless about mastering areas of their life and thus become overwhelmed by anxiety. Headache sufferers may say things to themselves like, "This is a pain in the neck"; "This gives me a headache"; "I can't cope."

This is not to imply that negative self-talk and poor attitudes about health are the only causes of these and other maladies. There are also inherited tendencies that determine, for instance, why one child might develop ulcers and another suffer from headaches.

We now realize that so-called psychosomatic illnesses—including some of the physical problems listed above—are real illnesses that are not as dissimilar to conditions caused by viruses or bacteria as we once thought. While the word *psychosomatic* suggests bodily symptoms caused by mental or emotional disturbance, we now know that *all* physical conditions are affected to some degree by the mind and our outlook.

Children need help to develop attitudes that enhance their health and help them to overcome debilitating health problems.

USING SELF-TALK TO PROGRAM FOR HEALTH

MODELING

Think about how you approach various aspects of your life that relate directly to health. What kind of model do you provide in the following areas?

Food. Do you eat on the run? Do you overeat when you're upset or do you get so upset you can't eat? Is eating an issue in your house? Do you try hard to have balanced foods for snacks and meals? Do you demonstrate your own enjoyment of good food?

What do you say about eating? Do you say, "I need to eat good foods to keep up my energy"; "I always stop and sit down to eat because it helps me to feel fresh and relaxed. I take my time eating so that I can digest my food well"?

Or do you say, "I can't stop myself from eating things I love"; "I don't have time to eat"; "I have to grab something on the run"; "I eat constantly when I get upset"; "It's important to eat everything on your plate"?

The models you provide children about food and eating are

crucial to their health now and in the future. You can lecture all you want about the importance of eating right, but it is what you yourself do and say that children will remember and imitate. That's one of the reasons that obesity and other food-related problems tend to run in families.

Adults with good intentions often cause food-related problems inadvertently through their concern about children's nutrition. Children who feel pressured to eat usually resist. The intake of food is one area parents can't control. When parents insist that children eat, children can exercise some control by refusing. Anorexia is acting this out to the extreme, but of course the issues there are more complex.

Parents often use food to console children. But it's better for children to learn to deal with their emotions and talk themselves through crises in positive ways than to eat as a substitute for coping.

Children need to learn about nutrition, but they also need to learn to tell themselves positive things about the process of eating, and about food.

Exercise. Children develop their attitudes toward exercise, at least in part, through observing what adults do and say about the process.

What do you say about exercise? "I'm too tired to exercise"; "I'm a couch potato"; "I feel that I have more energy after I exercise"; "Exercise helps my mood"; "Sometimes, when I'm upset, I like to take a long walk."

Handling stress. How you handle stress has a strong influence on children's self-talk. If you feel overwhelmed and helpless much of the time, your children are likely to feel that way about the challenges in their lives, too. On the other hand, it isn't useful for your children to imagine that you never experience stress, because then they have no realistic model for learning to cope with it themselves. Whenever you talk to your children about the anxieties you feel (a new job, moving), include statements about how you are coping. In that way, you provide a positive model for handling stress.

General attitude toward health. Think about how you talk about your health in general. Do you frequently complain about being tired? Do you see yourself as someone who catches every cold that comes by?

Research has shown that beliefs about health affect one's susceptibility to infection. Talking about health and expectations for good health in positive ways programs a person to resist disease and rally his energy.

It is important for children as well as adults to pay attention to bodily cues and respond to them appropriately. But complaining about health can actually program one to expect to be sick longer, or to get sick more often.

The model you provide should give your child the idea that she should pay attention to her physical symptoms and act appropriately, but that she shouldn't succumb to every ache and pain, or use complaints to get out of responsibilities.

For example, Alice wasn't feeling very well, so she told her children she was going to lie down and take a nap. At dinner she said that she still wasn't feeling great, but that she had to finish a report for work. If she had really been sick, as opposed to just feeling a little "off," she would have stayed in bed. By recognizing her susceptibility to illness and taking care of herself immediately, she was able to provide a coping model for her children. What she was saying to them was, "My health is important, but so is my work. If I think I can take care of myself and get my work done, that's what I'll do." That's a self-statement that we would like a child to make to himself in a similar situation.

Some of the attitudes outlined earlier in this chapter are also important when we think about the examples we present. For instance, people who can laugh at themselves when they make a mistake and see the humor in the world around them present better models of handling stress than people who take themselves too seriously.

Children also need to see how adults reach out to others in times of need; how parents actively confront problems instead of seeing themselves as victims; and how grown-ups stay involved by having interests and being interested in what goes on around them. Part of modeling health is presenting a picture of enthusiasm for life and reflecting that in what you say and do.

It is desirable to model a positive image about health. People who care for themselves and expect good health are more likely to experience it.

LISTEN TO WHAT YOUR CHILD SAYS ABOUT HIS HEALTH

Pediatricians have noticed that because of our hectic, busy lives, children's complaints often go unheeded. The child who complains of chronic stomachaches or headaches or who seems to be tired all the time may be urged to grin and bear it if he is not really sick. Often this advice is given because parents don't know what else to do, not because they don't care.

Parents may also be hesitant to give attention to these complaints because they wonder if children are using them to try to get out of school. A child may cry over a sore throat in the morning and feel fine by afternoon—and in the meantime her mother has lost a whole day of work.

A different way to think about these problems is to see the child's complaint as a form of self-talk. The symptom may or may not be real, but it expresses what a child feels he needs: time off, or help dealing with challenges he faces in some area of his life.

Everyone needs breaks sometimes to recoup from stressful situations. Illness is one way that people give themselves permission to take time out of their routines. Parents shouldn't be unduly solicitous with a child, or let him stay home over every little thing. But they need to pay attention to symptoms and what these say about his life.

What your child says about a particular problem can guide you in helping her to feel more in control of what's happening to her.

One seven-year-old complained frequently that her stomach hurt. She also asked questions about her grandmother, who, because of an illness, had just come to stay in her home. The pediatrician said the problem was psychosomatic, since he couldn't find anything physically wrong with the child. But he pointed out that that didn't mean it wasn't real. Her stomach probably did hurt. Her mother realized that the stress of having her sick grandmother living with them was causing the stomachaches. She started to encourage her daughter to talk about her feelings and she gave her a little extra nurturing, and the symptoms gradually disappeared.

When you tune in to a child's self-talk, you can often understand the underlying anxieties that are causing him physical problems.

PINPOINT REASONS FOR ONGOING PHYSICAL PROBLEMS

Children who have continuing physical complaints need help. A child who gets a stomachache every day before school and wants to stay home, or a teenager who always wants a note to be excused from phys ed because of a headache, shouldn't be told that he or she is faking it. First, they should be checked by a physician. If no physical problem is found, you can assume that the complaint is primarily caused by anxiety, fear, or other negative emotions. Begin to talk to the child about what he or she is feeling.

Sometimes a parent, teacher, or friendly adult can help a child learn to reduce her anxiety and the symptoms it causes just by talking to her. But if the problem is severe and of long duration, the child may benefit from seeing a child therapist, who can help her unravel the feelings that are causing her physical distress. Getting a youngster help with chronic physical problems is important because the problem itself affects her self-image and reinforces the idea that she can't cope.

HELP HIM RELAX

Once a child pinpoints a specific problem area such as the head, shoulders, stomach, or neck, you can help him concentrate on that part of the body and learn how to prevent tension before there's a problem. For instance, have him close his eyes and visualize his shoulders (if that's where he hurts); ask him to imagine breathing into his shoulders and letting his shoulders relax a little more each time he exhales, as if the breathing is taking the tension with it.

When a child learns such a technique he also needs to tell himself that he can use it in any situation, and that it will be effective. Giving himself the strong suggestion that the exercise will work makes its success more probable.

CHANGING SELF-TALK

When a child gets a stomachache before a test or a headache before a sports event, you might introduce the idea of changing his self-talk to help him reduce his discomfort and perhaps produce a better performance. For example, you might say, "When I'm nervous about doing something, my stomach twists and turns sometimes. I tell myself that I'm really nervous and then it makes me feel more nervous. But then I tell myself that I can handle this just fine and I say that my stomach can relax because I don't need to be upset. Have you ever tried that?"

You can even teach children to talk to parts of their bodies. Since the body is so responsive to what we say to ourselves, this is one way you can teach a child to program himself to feel better instead of worse. You might say, "Sometimes, when my stomach is upset, I talk to it and say, 'You don't need to feel tight and all knotted up. You can relax.' Then I picture my stomach relaxing and I try to help it relax."

Affirmations

Affirmations about health are particularly important because they can affect body chemistry in some profound ways.

Here are some examples of positive affirmations about health:

"I have all the energy I need and I feel good."
"I like my body just the way it is."
"I am healthy and strong."
"My body can fight off infection. I can picture the antibodies I need doing their job."
"I can handle this challenge and enjoy doing it."

Challenging negative self-talk

Once children have tuned in to the negative statements they make to themselves about health, they can learn to challenge that self-talk. Here are some examples.

Negative voice:

"You're going to be late. You'll never make it on time."

Challenge:

"Better to be a few minutes late than to have my stomach in knots when I get there."

Negative voice:

"You don't have time to eat."

Challenge:

"I'm not going to skip lunch or I'll be exhausted and hungry later on when I need energy."

Negative voice:

"You don't need to sleep. If you want to get the best grade in the class, you'd better stay up and get everything perfect."

Challenge:

"I don't have to be perfect. I won't be able to concentrate if I don't get any sleep. All I can do is my best."

Negative voice:

"Better do this test as fast as you can, or you're not going to make it."

Challenge:

"I don't have to get tense. Breathe deeply, slow down, and do this calmly."

Negative voice:

"You don't have time to rest. Maybe you'll get lucky and get sick and be able to stay home."

Challenge:

"I don't have to get sick to rest. I can rest when I need it and stay healthy."

SELF-TALK AND VISUALIZATION

Show children pictures of the insides of their bodies and explain the ways different internal processes work so that they can picture how the body miraculously fights off disease and functions in balanced and harmonious ways.

Then experiment with different forms of visualization. For example, have a child picture his white blood cells fighting off infection. He can have fun picturing them as armies fighting off an invader. He can talk to himself about the battle and how his armies will come out victorious.

Visualization, in conjunction with self-talk, is a powerful tool for programming health. It helps the child's mind to work in harmony with his body to create the reality that he wants.

CONCLUSION

Attitudes and what one says to oneself are strong determinants of health and susceptibility to illness. Many of these attitudes develop in childhood. As a parent or adult working with children, you need to be especially aware of the model you provide. How do you handle food, exercise, stress, and general health issues?

Once you tune in to a child's negative self-talk and outlooks that cause stress and poor health, you can help him change them by teaching him how to relax, visualize, make positive affirmations, and challenge negative self-talk.

Conclusion
...

The potential for changing ourselves through self-talk is vast. As a parent, grandparent, teacher, child therapist, coach, or anyone else who is interested in the growth of children, you can participate in breakthroughs in development by exploring the power of self-talk.

The future depends on each person's offering the best he can to the world. And that is made possible through self-knowledge and the will to become all that he is capable of being.

If people can convince themselves through self-talk to throw off limited visions of what they can be and of what the future can hold, then they can take a step forward in the evolution of human consciousness. We can begin to program ourselves for the unknown—for a life so full, productive, and positive that it can't yet be envisioned.

This expanded view will affect every arena of life: learning, work, play, creativity, love, relationships, child-rearing, physical and mental health, relaxation, and the enjoyment of life.

As authors, we are aware that people often read books, try out the ideas for a while, and then discard them. We hope that you will continue to experiment with self-talk. You might try that experimentation in various areas of your child's life or in your own life. You might try it as remedy for certain classroom discipline problems if you are a teacher or for certain types of emotional problems if you are a child therapist. It is your interest and effort that counts. Through your exploration, and the continued exploration of those like you, it is possible to change the way people view their own capabilities, and to create a larger vision.

BIBLIOGRAPHY

Bach, George, and Tarbet, Laura. *The Inner Enemy*. New York: Berkley Publishing, 1985.

Benson, Herbert. *The Relaxation Response*. New York: Morrow, 1975.

Bernard, Michael E., and Joyce, Marie R. *Rational-Emotive Therapy with Children and Adolescents*. New York: John Wiley and Sons, 1984.

Butler, Pamela E. *Talking to Yourself: Learning the Language of Self-Support*. San Francisco: Harper & Row, 1981.

Carson, Richard D. *Taming Your Gremlin*. New York: Harper & Row, 1983.

Cousins, Norman. *Anatomy of an Illness: The Healing Power of Humor*. New York: Norton, 1979.

Davis, Martha; Eshelman, Elizabeth Robbins; and McKay, Matthew. *The Relaxation and Stress Reduction Handbook*. Oakland, Calif.: New Harbinger Publications, 1982.

Fraiberg, Selma. *The Magic Years*. New York: Macmillan, 1959.

Gardner, Richard A. *The Talking, Feeling, and Doing Game*. Cresskill, N.J.: Creative Therapeutics, 1973.

——— *Therapeutic Communication with Children: The Mutual Story-telling Technique*. New York: Aronson, 1971.

Griswold, Bob. "Self-Image for Children." *The Love Tapes*. Edina, Minn.: Effective Learning Systems.

Grollman, E. A. *Explaining Death to Children*. Boston: Beacon Press, 1967.

Hauck, P. A., *The Rational Management of Children*. New York: Libra Publishers, 1967.

Helmstetter, Shad. *What to Say When You Talk to Your Self*. New York: Simon and Schuster, 1986.

Holt, John. *How Children Fail*. New York: Delacorte, 1982.

Kendall, Philip, and Braswell, Lauren. *Cognitive-Behavioral Therapy for Impulsive Children*. New York: Gilford Press, 1985.

Kent, Fraser. *Nothing to Fear: Coping with Phobias*. Garden City, N.Y.: Doubleday, 1977.

Lupin, Mini. *Peace, Harmony, Awareness: A Relaxation Program for Children*. Austin, Tex.: Learning Concepts, 1977.

Moseley, Ellis A., and Wolfe, J. L. *How To Raise an Emotionally Healthy Child*. New York: Crown Publishers, 1966.

Pelletier, Kenneth. *Mind as Healer, Mind as Slayer*. New York: Delacorte, 1977.

Ross, Helen. *Fears of Children*. Chicago: Science Research Associates, 1970.

Schaefer, Charles E., and Millman, Howard L. *How To Help Children with Common Problems*. New York: Litton Educational Publishing, 1981.

Siegel, Bernie S. *Love, Medicine, and Miracles*. New York: Harper and Row, 1988.

Simonton, Carl and Stephanie, *Getting Well Again*. Los Angeles: Tarcher, 1978.

Tutko, Thomas. *Sports Psyching: Playing Your Best Game All the Time*. Los Angeles: Tarcher, 1976.

Vygotsky, Lev. *Thought and Language*. Cambridge, Mass.: MIT Press, 1986.

Walker, C. E. *Learn to Relax*. Englewood Cliffs, N.J.: Prentice-Hall, 1975.

Wertsch, James. *Vygotsky and the Social Formation of the Mind*. Cambridge, Mass.: Harvard University Press, 1985.

Wolman, Benjamin. *Children's Fears*. New York: Grosset & Dunlap, 1978.

Young, H. S. *A Rational Counseling Primer*. New York: Institute for Rational Living, 1974.

Zilbergeld, Bernie, and Lazarus, Arnold A. *Mind Power*. Boston: Little, Brown, 1987.

INDEX

Abstract thinking, 102, 155, 165
Achievement. *See* Learning and studying; Motivation; Remembering past successes
Active engagement and health, 177–178
Adolescents, 9, 22–23, 60–61, 79, 88, 102–103, 153–172, 179
Adult-child relationships during adolescence, 159–161
Affirmations. *See* Positive affirmations
Aggressiveness, 5, 25, 52, 58, 62, 69–71, 76, 117, 128–130, 145–147, 180
Anatomy of an Illness (Cousins), 176
Anger, 20, 21, 25–26, 33, 49–52, 56–74, 97, 128–130, 140–142, 179, 180. *See also* Negotiating conflicts
Anorexia, 179–180, 182
Anxiety, 20, 39–42, 84, 107, 116–117, 180, 183. *See also* Fears; Stress
Assertiveness, 144–147
Athletics
  psychology of, 119–123
  self-talk and, 22, 32–33, 44–45, 82–85, 114–126
Attention span, 103
Autogenic training, 40–42
Avoidance and fear, 92

Bach, George, 14
Bedtime, 8, 31, 86–87. *See also* Fears
Belief system and illness, 173
Blaming statements, 144. *See also* Criticism
Bloomfield, Stephen, 176
Books
  handling social situations and, 149–150
  self-help, 2–3
Boundary problems and anger, 63–64
Brain function, 3, 5–6
Breathing to relax, 40, 119–120

Bulimia, 179–180
Bully, the, 25, 128–130. *See also* Aggressiveness

Carelessness and learning, 100–101
Catastrophizing, 165
Challenge of sports, 116–117
Challenges to negative voices
  adolescent friendships and, 164–167
  anger and, 68–69
  disapproval and rejection and, 141–143
  fear and, 83–88
  health and, 188–189
  how to use, 33–36
  initiating new relationships and, 138–139
  learning and, 109–110
  negotiating conflicts and, 145–147
  overgeneralizing and, 143
  sports and, 124–125
  See also Inner voices
Child development. *See* Development of children, phases of
Childhood illnesses and self-talk, 179–181
Clinging child, 1–2, 4, 85–86
Cognitive development of children, 101–104, 117, 155–156
Colds, 174, 176, 179, 183
Colitis, 180
Communication problems and anger, 64
Concentration, 100, 117, 120–124
Confidence, 22, 28, 33, 38, 44–45, 91
Conflicts, negotiating, 143–147, 149. *See also* Anger
Controlling talk, 23–26. *See also* Discipline
Coping
  model of, 183
  nurturing talk and, 24, 26–27
  statements of, 88
Cousins, Norman, 173, 176

Creativity, 102
Criticism, 33, 43, 118, 142
Crying and health, 176
Cue words, 32–33

Dark, fear of, 86–87
Dating, 22, 156–158, 162–163, 170
Deep breathing, 40
Definition of self-talk, 2–11
Development of children, phases of
  adolescence and, 154–157
  anger and, 60–61
  fear and, 79–81
  health and, 178–179
  learning and, 101–104
  self-talk and, 8–9
  social skills and, 132–135
  sports and, 117
"Die" messages, 174
Disapproval, dealing with, 139–143, 148–149. *See also* Peer pressure
Discipline, 23–26, 62–64, 82

Eating habits
  disorders of, 179–180, 182
  modeling, 181–182
Egocentric speech, 6, 17
Egocentric thinking, 102–103, 132
Elementary-school children, 9, 42, 60, 94, 102, 117, 134–135, 178–179
Emotions and health, 173–174, 180–181
Empathy, 129, 133
Empowering words, 18–19. *See also* Positive affirmations
Exceptional Cancer Patients, 173
Exercise, physical, 182

Fears, 5, 8, 21, 49–51, 75–93, 94–96, 107, 138, 180
Filtering, 18, 34
Flu, 179
Focus and sports, 123–124
Fraiberg, Selma, 76
Friends, making and keeping, 5, 21, 22, 35, 127–152, 153–172, 177
Frustration tolerance, 101, 140–141. *See also* Anger; Negotiating conflicts; Self-control
Future talk, 24, 28–29

Games
  presenting self-talk as, 10
  "The Talking, Feeling, and Doing Game," 89, 150
  "What If?," 89
  "What Would You Say to Yourself?," 150
Getting Well Again (Simonton), 177–178

Headaches, 180, 184, 186–187
Health, 27, 57, 115, 173–190
Helmstetter, Shad, 2–3, 5, 23
Helplessness, 18, 25, 34, 59, 76, 78, 84, 157, 176–177, 180, 182
Heroes, 45, 163
Holt, John, 94–95
Horton, Paul, 2
How Children Fail (Holt), 94–95
How to Help Children with Common Problems (Schaefer and Millman), 79
Humor, 13, 175–176, 184
Hypothetical situations, using
  anger and, 66–67
  fear and, 89–90
  impulse control and, 130
  learning and, 109
  social interaction and, 148–149

Illnesses of childhood, 179–181. *See also* Health
Imagery, 42, 102
Impulse control, 9, 25–26, 70, 129, 130, 134–135, 140, 142
Individuation, 160
Initiating new relationships, 135–139, 148, 167–168, 170
Inner Enemy, The (Bach), 14
Inner voices, 13–17, 19, 22, 58, 99–101. *See also* Challenges to negative voices
Instructor, voice of. *See* Self-instruction
Intuition, 10, 102

Language development, 6, 17
Laughter and health, 175–176, 184
Learning and studying, 5, 21, 34, 44, 77–78, 94–113. *See also* Tests, fear of
Listening. *See* Observing self-talk

"Live" messages, 174
Love, Medicine, and Miracles (Siegel), 173
Love Tapes, The (Effective Learning Systems), 42

Magic Years, The (Fraiberg), 76
Mental rehearsal
  adolescent friendships and, 168–169, 171
  anger and, 71
  fear and, 91
  how to use, 47–49
  social situations and, 150–151
  sports and, 122, 124
Millman, Howard, 79
Mistakes, 85, 111–112, 125
Modeling positive self-talk
  adolescent friendships and, 162–163
  anger and, 62–63, 140–141
  fear and, 82
  health and, 181–184
  how to use, 8, 23–29
  initiating new relationships and, 135–136
  learning and, 104, 106
  negotiating conflicts and, 144–145
  rejection and disapproval and, 139–141
  sports and, 118–119
Motivation, 5, 9, 44, 97–101, 121
Mutual storytelling, 89–90

Name-calling, 144, 146. *See also* Criticism
Negative voices. *See* Challenges to negative voices
Negotiating conflicts, 143–147, 149. *See also* Anger
Nelson, Byron, 119
New situations, fear of, 87–88
Nicklaus, Jack, 122
Nurturing and coping talk, 24, 26–27

Observing self-talk, 12–20, 63, 184–185
Overgeneralizing, 18, 142–143, 164–165

Panic, 84, 119
Paradoxical intention, 92–93
Parents, role of during adolescence, 159–161

Passive children and conflict, 145–147
Peer pressure, 156, 158–159, 165–166. *See also* Rejection, fear of
Pelletier, Kenneth, 178
Performance, fear of, 81–82, 84–85, 89, 114–126. *See also* Athletics, self-talk and; Tests, fear of
Phobias, 5, 78
Playacting to overcome fear, 80
Positive affirmations
  adolescent friendships and, 163–164
  anger and, 67–68
  fear and, 82–83
  health and, 187–188
  how to use, 30–32
  initiating new relationships and, 136–137
  learning and, 108–109
  negotiating conflicts and, 145
  rejection and disapproval and, 141
  sports and, 124
Praise, 51, 71–73
Predictions. *See* Future talk
Preschoolers, 5–6, 8–9, 57–58, 60, 63, 79, 81, 94, 101–103, 132–133
Problem-solving strategies
  anger and, 59, 69–71
  fear and, 90–91
  how to use, 51–53
Psychic stress, 81. *See also* Stress
Psychology of sports, 119–123
Psychosomatic illnesses, 180–181, 185
Psychotherapy. *See* Therapy and self-talk
Punishment. *See* Discipline
Put-downs, 144, 146. *See also* Criticism

Rehearsal. *See* Mental rehearsal
Rejection, fear of, 139–143, 148–149, 169. *See also* Peer pressure
Relationships. *See* Adult-child relationships during adolescence; Friends, making and keeping
Relaxation, 30, 39–42, 45, 48, 51, 73, 90, 102, 107, 116–119, 186–187
Remembering past successes, 43–48, 103, 111
Resistance to discipline, 64
Retention, poor, 100
Role of self-talk. *See* Self-talk, role of

Role-playing, 71, 91, 150–151, 158, 168–169, 171

Schaefer, Charles, 79
School. *See* Learning and studying; Tests, fear of
Schoolchildren. *See* Elementary-school children
Self-control, 9, 25–26, 70, 129, 130, 134–135, 140, 142. *See also* Anger
Self-help books, 2–3
"Self-Image for Children," 42
Self-instruction, 99–101, 106, 167–168, 170
Self-talk, definition of, 2–11
Self-talk, role of
 adolescent friendships and, 157–159
 anger and, 57–59
 fear and, 76–78
 health and, 175–178
 learning and motivation and, 97–101
 relationships and, 128–131
Self-talk, steps for learning, 12–37, 38–55
Separation, fear of, 1–2, 4, 85–86
Sharing your experience
 anger and, 61
 fear and, 81–82
 initiating new relationships and, 136
 introducing self-talk and, 21
 learning and, 104–106
 sports and, 118
Shyness, 52–53, 129, 130, 135–137, 157–158, 169
Siebert, Albert, 175
Siegal, Bernie S., 173–174
Simonton, Carl and Stephanie, 177–178
Smith, Walter, 176
Social interactions. *See* Friends, making and keeping
Social skills, development of, 132–135
Social support and health, 177
Soskis, David, 32
Sports Psyching (Tutko), 107, 116–117
Sports
 psychology of, 119–123
 self-talk and, 22, 32–33, 44–45, 82–85, 114–126

Steps to learning self-talk, 12–37, 38–55
Stomachaches, 114–115, 180, 184–187
Storytelling, mutual, 89–90
Stress, 3, 13–14, 26–27, 39–42, 73, 81, 107, 114–115, 119, 174–177, 179–180, 182–185. *See also* Anxiety
Stress inoculation, 49–51, 73
Studying. *See* Learning and studying
Substituting good talk for bad, 29–36
Successes, remembering, 43–48, 103, 111

"Talking, Feeling, and Doing Game," 89, 150
Tantrums, 56, 60, 72
Teaching talk, 23, 24
Teenagers. *See* Adolescents
Temper. *See* Anger
Temperaments, 13
Tension, releasing, 39–42. *See also* Relaxation; Stress
Tests, fear of, 32, 34–35, 43–44, 48, 84–85, 89, 108. *See also* Learning and studying
Therapy and self-talk, 11, 186
Thoughts and health, 173–174, 180–181
Tiredness, 184
Tutko, Thomas, 107, 116–117, 120, 123

Ulcers, 180
Unknown, fear of the, 87–88

Visualization, 6, 38–55, 108–109, 189–190
Voices. *See* Inner voices

Wetting and soiling, 179
"What If?" game, 89
"What if's," 165
What to Say When You Talk to Your Self (Helmstetter), 23
"What Would You Say to Yourself?" game, 150
Wizard, talking to the, 53–54